DISCIPLES ARE MADE NOT BORN

Helping Others Grow to Maturity in Christ

WALTER A. HENRICHSEN

Foreword by Howard G. Hendricks

David C Cook®

transforming lives together

DISCIPLES ARE MADE NOT BORN
Published by David C Cook
4050 Lee Vance View
Colorado Springs, CO 80918 U.S.A.

David C Cook Distribution Canada
55 Woodslee Avenue, Paris, Ontario, Canada N3L 3E5

David C Cook U.K., Kingsway Communications
Eastbourne, East Sussex BN23 6NT, England

The graphic circle C logo is a registered trademark of David C Cook.

Unless otherwise noted, Scripture quotations are from the King James Version of
the Bible. (Public Domain.) Other quotations are from the New American Standard
Bible (nasb), © Copyright The Lockman Foundation, 1960, 1977. All rights reserved.

Library of Congress Cataloging-in-Publication Data

Henrichsen, Walter A.
Disciples are made not born / by Walter Henrichsen..
p. cm.
ISBN 978-0-781438-83-4
eISBN 978-1-4347-0471-9
1. Christian life. 2. Evangelistic work. I. Title.
BV4501.2.H374 2002
296/.2

© 1974, 1988 by Walter A. Henrichsen

Editor: Craig Bubeck, Sr. Editor (over update)
Interior Design: Kelly Robinson
Cover Design: Kevin Keller, DesignConcepts
Cover Photo: © iStock

Printed in the United States of America
Second Edition 1988

14 15 16 17 18

021213

CONTENTS

FOREWORD

"Make disciples" is the mandate of the Master (Matt. 28:19-20). We may ignore it, but we cannot evade it.

Our risen Christ left this legacy—the magna carta of the church. He provided both the model and the method. His life and death—recast the lives of men. He demonstrated that you have not done anything until you have changed the lives of men.

"Follow Me," He urged His men. And then that staggering assurance: "Lo, I am with you always." Somehow we have forgotten that this promise is not a carte blanche; His promise is linked with a process. We cannot embrace the promise and ignore the process.

Much of the feverish and frustrating activity of the contemporary church is devoid of relevance and fulfillment. Entertainment, not education, is our program. Laymen are disenchanted. They are looking for an involvement with eternal bite. C.S. Lewis said it: "All that is not eternal is eternally out of date."

Disciples Are Made—Not Born is not a collection of dry, doctrinal dust, but an eminently practical and provocative cud to chew on. The writer constantly hits the nail on the head.

Walt Henrichsen is no mere theorist. Long associated with The Navigators—an organization committed to disciple-making—he has probed the Scriptures persistently, and has presented effectively the results of his study and experience.

He also writes out of the reality of family life. He and his wife, Leette, have had the joy of discipling four active children. And they have known the heartache of losing their older son to leukemia.

Here is a primer on discipleship, commended to the one who wants to walk where Christ walked and sustain a ministry of multiplication. These pages fill an urgent need in our generation when the battle is for the minds and hearts of men.

"Everyone, after he has been fully trained, will be like his teacher," our Lord avowed (Luke 6:40, NASB). This book invites you to take His yoke upon you and learn of Him.

—HOWARD G. HENDRICKS
Professor of Christian Education
Dallas Theological Seminary

Chapter 1

THE KIND OF PERSON GOD USES

When Jesus Christ voluntarily gave His life on the cross some 2,000 years ago, He did not die for a cause. He died for people. During His ministry on earth, He "ordained twelve, that they should be with him, and that he might send them forth to preach" (Mark 3:14). Just before His death on Calvary, Jesus prayed for His men (see John 17). Over 40 times in that prayer, He referred to His twelve disciples.

During His brief ministry on earth, Jesus had the world on His heart, but He saw the world through the eyes of His men. Prior to His ascension, He gave to these men what is commonly referred to as the Great Commission. As recorded in Matthew 28:19, Jesus charged them to take the Gospel throughout the world by making disciples.

Jesus had world vision. He expected His men to have world vision. Jesus expected them to see the world through the disciples that they would produce, just as He had seen the world through the twelve men He had raised up. His vision of reaching the world through the use of multiplying disciples is not found in an obscure passage in the Bible it is a theme that pulsates from page to page.

It was obviously the thought that was on the apostle Paul's heart as he wrote his "last will and testament" to his son in the faith, Timothy. Let's briefly analyze 2 Timothy 2:2: "And the things that thou hast heard of me among many witnesses, the same commit thou to faithful men, who shall be able to teach others also."

Thou indicates the importance of the individual. At Jesus' meeting with Peter, He said, according to John 1:42, "Thou art Simon … thou shalt be called Cephas." (You are Simon, you will become a rock.) When Jesus saw Peter, He did not see him as he was but as he would someday be. There is tremendous potential in the life of one man.

Thou …me indicates the importance of personal relationships, of mutual confidence and trust built up through years of laboring together. When Paul wrote from prison to the church at Philippi, he said that because he was unable to visit them, he would send Timothy, his son in the faith. In essence what he said was, "When Timothy arrives, it will be as though I myself were present."

Many years earlier Paul had seen the potential in this young man from Asia Minor and decided to invest his life in him.

Commit suggests transmitting something from one person to another. It indicates the deposit of a sacred trust. Paul is saying to Timothy, "You are my disciple. This is the relationship that exists between you and me. Now transmit this as a disciple-maker to other disciples."

When we invest in the lives of other people, we transmit not only what we know but, more importantly, what we are. Each of us becomes like the people with whom we associate. I am sure that if we could meet Paul and Timothy, we would find them similar in many respects.

Later Paul wrote to him, "But thou hast fully known my doctrine, manner of life, purpose, faith, longsuffering, charity, patience, persecutions" (2 Tim. 3:10-11). This gives a synopsis of what was committed to Timothy by Paul and what in turn was to be committed by Timothy to faithful men.

Faithful men—Discipling stands or falls with these two little words. Solomon, that wise king of ancient Israel, said, "Most men will proclaim every one his own goodness: but a faithful man who can find?" (Prov. 20:6) Faithful men and women have always been in short supply. God still seeks them out. "For the eyes of the LORD run to and fro throughout the whole earth, to shew himself strong in the behalf of *them* whose heart *is* perfect toward him" (2 Chron. 16:9).

Teach others also—This is where the discipling process begins to pick up a head of steam. We are now in the fourth generation. We began with Paul, then Timothy, then faithful men, and finally, others also. Teaching others cannot be done solely through a classroom situation. It entails the imparting of a life—the same in-depth transmission that occurred between Paul and Timothy.

This is a multiplicative process. While the faithful men are teaching others also, Timothy is in the process of raising up more faithful men, who shall be able to teach others also. Implementing this vision of multiplying disciples constitutes the only way Christ's commission can ever ultimately be fulfilled. Other ministries and approaches can augment it but never replace it.

Dawson Trotman, founder of The Navigators, used to say, "Activity is no substitute for production. Production is no substitute for reproduction." Whatever ministry we are engaged in, it ought to be reproductive.

We have already pointed out that the key to this disciple-making ministry is faithful men and women. What are the qualifications for a faithful person? What qualities of godliness must be characteristic of his life? Let's mentally digest a few essential traits of the person who wants to qualify as "a faithful man."

He Has Adopted the Same Objective in Life that God Sets Forth in the Scriptures.

Jesus said, "But seek ye first the kingdom of God, and his righteousness; and all these things shall be added unto you" (Matt. 6:33). Rarely did the Lord Jesus ask people to seek something, but here He suggests we seek two things which are to become the twofold objective of every believer: His kingdom and His righteousness.

Notice that Jesus does not say to seek money or a wife or a dozen other things that could easily occupy our attention. Rather, He is saying that if we seek His kingdom and His righteousness, He will assume responsibility for meeting every other need in our lives.

A friend of mine is a lawyer in a prestigious law firm. Year after year he had the highest earnings in the firm, but his colleagues would not make him a senior partner. The reason was that all these men gave their lives, their time, and their energy to the firm. But because my friend was a Christian, he did not feel that the practice of law rated that high on his priority list. He was a superb lawyer and did a good job—as the financial records indicated. But his objective was Matthew 6:33. Being a lawyer was a means to an end, not an end in itself. I believe it was because of his commitment that God entrusted him with so much success.

Whatever your vocation is, it must never be your life objective; for your vocation, no matter how noble it may be, is, in the final analysis, temporal. The Scriptures teach us that we are to give our lives to the eternal and not to the temporal. A faithful man is a man who has chosen eternal objectives for his life.

He Is Willing to Pay Any Price to Have the Will of God Fulfilled in His Life.

This is a crucial issue. After instructing Timothy to commit to faithful people the things that Timothy had learned from him, Paul goes on to say, "Suffer hardship with *me*, as a good soldier of Christ Jesus. No soldier in active service entangles himself in the affairs of everyday life, so that he may please the one who enlisted him as a soldier" (2 Tim. 2:3-4 NASB). Having committed himself to God's objective, the faithful man steadfastly resists becoming ensnared in the world's glittering attractions.

Let me ask you: Is there anything between you and God? Are there any little pet sins that you have been unwilling to confess and forsake? Any areas that you have not put under His control? How about your finances? The question is not how much money you have in the bank, but rather who has the power to draw on your account? Do all of your financial assets belong to Jesus Christ? Do you know what it means to give sacrificially? And by that I mean to give what you know from a human perspective you cannot afford.

How about "things"? Do your possessions play an inordinate role in your life? Paul says, "For many walk, of whom I have told you often, and now tell you even weeping, *that they are* the enemies of the cross of Christ: whose end *is* destruction, whose God *is their* belly, and whose glory is in their shame, who mind earthly things" (Phil. 3:18-19). The Bible says that people "who mind earthly things" are enemies of the cross of Christ.

All that you hold dear to yourself—your family, your health, your dreams, your aspirations and goals—must be held with an open hand. If you desire to fulfill God's will for your life irrespective of the price, the sum total of all that makes up you must belong to Jesus Christ. He must be free to do with you and take from you as He pleases. You need not open your hand to God with a sense of fear, for God loves you with a perfect love and has your best interests at heart. But having said that, the faithful person is one who is willing to pay any price to have the will of God accomplished in his life.

He Has a Love for the Word of God.

The Prophet Jeremiah said, "Thy words were found, and I did eat them; and thy word was unto me the joy and rejoicing of mine heart: for I am called by thy name, O LORD God of hosts" (Jer. 15:16). Do you have an insatiable appetite for the Word of God? Do you crave it like you crave food? Are you in submission to the authority of the Word of God? Or do you pick and choose what to believe and obey?

A carpenter whom I have known for years averages 10 hours each week in Bible study. This man has never gone to college or

Bible school. He is not a learned scholar, but for him the Scriptures have a place of priority. I believe it was St. Jerome who said that the Scriptures are shallow enough for a babe to come and drink without fear of drowning and deep enough for theologians to swim in without ever touching the bottom.

One day I was in the office of a surgeon. In the course of his training, he had to master the contents of scores of books. If he were to operate on me or one of my family, I would certainly want it that way! As I thought about this, it occurred to me that, as Christ's disciples, we really only have one Book we must master—the Bible. Yet, when I talk to people about investing five hours each week in Bible study and memorizing a couple of verses a week, they look at me as though some monstrous demand were being made on them.

What is your Scripture intake? Do you have a regular Bible reading program? Are you systematically studying the Scriptures? Is your craving for the Bible so great that it is impossible to satisfy?

He Has a Servant Heart.

Jesus once reminded His disciples that nonChristians enjoy being served and exercising authority over others. In contrast to this He said, "But it shall not be so among you: but whosoever will be great among you, let him be your minister; and whosoever will be chief among you, let him be your servant: even as the Son of man came not to be ministered unto, but to minister, and to give his life a ransom for many" (Matt. 20:26-28).

The motto of the British Royal Military Academy is "Serve to Lead." This is the same truth Jesus was seeking to communicate to His disciples when He washed their feet (see John 13). If, as their Lord, He washed their feet, they ought to be willing to do the same for others.

A person may try to recruit others to help him accomplish his vision. The disciple-maker, however, seeks to invest his life in another to help that person accomplish his own vision.

He Puts No Confidence in the Flesh.

The Scriptures emphasize this principle often. Paul said, "But we had the sentence of death in ourselves, that *we should not trust in ourselves,* but in God who raiseth the dead" (2 Cor. 1:9). Again he said, "For I know that in me (that is, in my flesh), dwelleth no good thing" (Rom. 7:18).

Worldliness and having confidence in the flesh are very closely related, for *worldliness* can be defined as "living as though you had no need for God." For example, to leave for work in the morning without first spending time with the Lord to me indicates having a tremendous amount of confidence in oneself. It is equivalent to saying, "I can run my life today without an absolute dependence on God."

One of the ways of determining exactly how much confidence you have in the flesh is to take an inventory of the number of times *you* come into your own conversation. How often do you talk about how great you are and the things you have done?

He Does Not Have an Independent Spirit.

There is a great deal of talk today about "doing your own thing." In this antiauthoritarian society in which we live, the attitude is, "Don't let people tell you what to do." Accomplishing the work of

God, however, is a team effort. It is done in concert with like-minded brothers and sisters in the faith. There is no room in the life of the disciple for a loner's attitude the kind of attitude that says, "If it is not done my way, then I'm not going to do it at all."

A young man once told me, "I will listen to what God has to say to me, but I will not learn from other people." To have such an attitude is to live in self-deception. People are often God's instruments to communicate to other people. God is looking for faithful people who are willing to subjugate their own ideas for the sake of the team.

He Has a Love for People.

The apostle John said, "Herein is love, not that we loved God, but that he loved us, and sent his Son *to be* the propitiation for our sins" (1 John 4:10). To be godly is to be God-like. To be like God is to love people, because God loves people.

I remember reading a "Peanuts" cartoon in which Charlie Brown said, "I love the world. I think the world is wonderful. It's people I can't stand." Yet, people are the reason Jesus invaded human history. He came to redeem people. That is what the Gospel is all about. The disciple is one who is involved in the lives of people. The faithful person has a love for people.

He Does Not Allow Himself to Become Trapped in Bitterness.

The writer of Hebrews warns us to be watchful "lest any man fail of the grace of God; lest any root of bitterness springing up trouble *you,* and thereby many be defiled" (Heb. 12:15). The context of this verse is the giving and receiving of rebuke. Many a person has become bitter because someone pointed out a fault in his life. He takes the attitude, "Huh, who does he think he is, telling me about my sins? Why doesn't he take the beam out of his own eye before he takes the little speck of sawdust out of mine?"

As a young Christian, I remember hearing someone preach on this verse, and I jotted in the margin of my Bible next to it, "Bitterness comes as a result of real or supposed ill-treatment—it doesn't really matter which." Somebody may really wrong you, or you may just think that somebody wronged you. In either case, if you are not careful, it can cause you to become bitter.

A wise, old saint once said, "I will never allow another person to ruin my life by making me hate him."

The root of bitterness can come through a competitive spirit, a breakdown in communications between you and fellow Christians, or from feeling that you have gotten a raw deal. I believe more disciples become ineffective in the Christian life because of a root of bitterness than because of any other sin. Faithful Christians guard their hearts well in this critical area.

He Has Learned to Discipline His Life.

One of the most motivating passages of Scripture that I know was penned by the apostle Paul. "Do you not know that those who run in a race all run, but only one receives the prize? Run in such a way that you may win. And everyone who competes in the games exercises self-control in all things. They then do it to receive a perishable wreath, but we an imperishable. Therefore I run in such a way, as not without aim; I box in such a way, as not beating the air; but I buffet my body and make it my slave, lest possibly, after I have preached to others, I myself should be disqualified" (1 Cor. 9:24-27 NASB).

One day I sat down and meditated on what would be the most horrible thing that could happen to me as a Christian. The conclusion to which I came was that when I die, God would take me aside and say to me, "Henrichsen, let Me show you what your life could have been like *if only* you had done what I asked, *if only* you had been faithful to Me, *if only* you had disciplined your life and made it really count, as I wanted you to."

Have you learned to discipline yourself? Have you learned to say no to temptation? Maybe there is a habit that you have been unable to conquer. You know that the Spirit of God would like you to get victory, but you have done nothing about it, having rationalized that, "If God wants me to give up this habit, then He will have to give me the power to do it." Although this is true, it is avoiding the issue, because God has already given you the power. It has been made available to you through the Holy Spirit. All you need to do is appropriate it—and such appropriation requires discipline. Never blame God for your failure to do what you know is right.

It is the evening that you have set aside for Bible study, but you discover that one of your favorite programs is on television. So you rationalize by saying you will do the study some other time. Not only does the Bible study not get done, but you also stay up so late that night that you are unable to get up the next morning in time to fellowship alone with the Lord before going to work.

It is not the one or two isolated times of compromise that will make the difference. The problem is that once you make an exception, it is so easy to do it again, and again, and again. You sow a thought and reap an act. You sow an act and reap a habit. You sow a habit, and you reap an eternity.

It is evident that one does not become a "faithful person" by being a weekend Christian. The faithful person is one who has applied the Scriptures to every area of his life. The life of discipleship is a life of discipline—the two words come from the same root. A disciple is a disciplined person. Such a life is not easy, but God never promised us it would be. That it is not easy is clearly seen by the fact that there are so few faithful people around today.

The gold medal goes to the athlete who has worked hard, who has learned how to discipline himself, who has learned to say no to the myriad distractions that cross a person's life, who has a clear-cut objective and has resolved in his soul to stay with it until he accomplishes it. This is the kind of person God uses.

Chapter 2

JESUS AS LORD

One of the men on The Navigators staff is a Jamaican. Some years ago, he worked for a banana company near his hometown of Kingston, Jamaica. He was doing so well in the company that one day one of the executives invited him into his office to discuss his future.

After assessing the young man's potential, the executive said, "You have a great future with our company, with excellent prospects for rapid promotion. But we are looking for committed men. If you are going to be a success, I want you to know that you will have to give your life in exchange for bananas."

The young man thought about it for a few moments and decided that he could not sign away his life for bananas.

Lordship involves giving Jesus Christ the number one place above all the possible "bananas" in your life.

This chapter deals with four aspects involved in making Christ the Lord of our lives.

1. The fact that Jesus is Lord whether we want Him to be or not
2. Reasons we don't want to acknowledge Him as Lord
3. What it means to acknowledge Him as Lord
4. Why Jesus wants to be our Lord

Let's look at these, one at a time.

Jesus Is Lord Whether We Want Him to Be or Not.

Jesus Christ is the Creator of *all* things and "by the word of His power" He holds everything together. "For by him were all things created, that are in heaven, and that are in earth, visible and invisible, whether *they be* thrones, or dominions, or principalities, or powers: all things were created by him, and for him, and he is before all things, and by him all things consist. And he is the head of the body, the church: who is the beginning, the firstborn from the dead; that in all *things* he might have the preeminence" (Col. 1:16-18).

Have you ever considered how little of your life you control? Did you decide when you would be born? Or who your parents would be? Or in what country you would be born? Did you decide the color of your skin? your eyes? your hair? Did you decide your intelligence or your gifts and talents? How about your height—did you determine that? Or your appearance, whether you would be good looking or rather plain? The answer to all these questions is no. In every one of these areas and in many more, you have no say in the matter. Your vote counts for absolutely nothing!

Then at what point do you exercise control? The Bible suggests that you control a small but important part of your life, namely your will. Lordship has to do with your will. It involves surrendering it to Jesus Christ. It means that Jesus is Lord of all of you, not just part of you. In making this decision of the will, remember that He has control over most things that concern you, whether you like it or not.

Why We Don't Want to Acknowledge Him as Lord.

Though every person has his own reasons not to acknowledge Jesus as Lord, some reasons come up with remarkable frequency.

1. He may ask us to do something that we do not want to do.

Of course, He will. If this were not so, there would be no issue involved. When you make Jesus Christ Lord of your life, you can count on Him asking you to do things you would rather not do.

Abraham did not want to offer up Isaac as a sacrifice. Moses did not want to go before Pharaoh. Joseph did not want to spend all those years in prison. Jesus Christ did not want to go to the cross.

Nobody likes the cross. Nobody likes to die. Nobody likes to deny himself. But this is what lordship is all about. A disciple is a disciplined one. He is one who says no to what he wants in deference to what his Lord wants. The disciple does not pamper himself by satisfying his wants and desires in a self-gratifying fashion.

When Jesus Christ is Lord of your life, every area is under His jurisdiction—your thoughts, your actions, your plans, your vocation, your leisure time, and your life goal. All of these are under His lordship.

2. We think we know what is best for us.

Nothing could be farther from the truth. A child left alone would kill himself. He might eat the wrong things, or run out in the street, or grab hold of a sharp knife, or play with something equally dangerous. The parent must keep constant watch over his child. That is, the parent must be lord of the child's life. In fact, the law requires that this be so; and when the parent refuses to exercise such lordship, the courts hold him accountable.

When we reach physical maturity, however, we think that things suddenly change. This is where we make our mistake. A child left to himself will probably hurt himself. As mature adults, left to ourselves, we *do* hurt ourselves.

A group of scientists has warned that the United States has enough atomic warheads to destroy every human being on the face of the earth—the equivalent of one railroad boxcar load of dynamite for every man, woman, and child in the world. And this is to say nothing about the atomic warheads that other nations of the world have.

Have you ever thought about the fact that we hire policemen to watch over us to make sure that we don't do anything wrong? Yet, we have the audacity to say that we know what is best for our lives.

3. We are not sure that God has our best interests at heart.

If God wanted to make it hard on us, can you imagine what He could do? If He wanted to make us miserable and plague us with difficulties, He could make life absolutely intolerable.

One might argue that God does not want to get involved in our lives, but it is ridiculous to say that He wants to hurt us.

However, you cannot argue that Jesus Christ does not want to get involved in your life. The very issue of lordship revolves around the fact that He *does* want to get involved in your life. Listen to what He says through the Prophet Jeremiah. "'For I know the plans I have for you,' says the Lord. 'They are plans for good and not for evil, to give you a future and a hope'" (Jer. 29:11 TLB).

What It Means to Acknowledge Him as Lord

The implications of recognizing Jesus Christ as Lord are readily seen in the prayer He taught His disciples.

> "After this manner therefore pray ye: Our Father which art in heaven, Hallowed be thy name. Thy kingdom come. Thy will be done in earth, as *it is* in heaven. Give us this day our daily bread. And forgive us our debts, as we forgive our debtors. And lead us not into temptation, but deliver us from evil: For thine is the kingdom, and the power, and the glory, for ever. Amen." (Matt. 6:9–13)

Notice that the prayer begins, *Our Father.* Jesus did not instruct us to say, "My Father," but "Our Father." The disciple must be able to identify with people where they are, to sit where they sit. The disciple himself is not one who has arrived. On the contrary, he is a learner, a pilgrim, one who is on a quest to make his life all that God would have it be. Therefore, he must understand the needs and frailties of people.

Hallowed be thy name. Jesus did not pray that His name would be hallowed, but that the Father's name would be hallowed. Acknowledging His lordship means surrendering your name.

Are you interested in making a name for yourself? Are you desirous of being recognized by people? Are your life goals self-serving—to make a great scientific discovery, do well in business, be married to an important person? To have Jesus as your Lord means to desire that His name, not yours, be hallowed.

Thy kingdom come. God's desire is to rule here on earth just as He rules in heaven.

He is in the process of building His kingdom. Are you untiringly laboring to build the kingdom of Christ, or are you busy building your own little kingdom? In your church, is it your Sunday school class, your board of deacons or elders, your building project, your missionary program? Do these things get you attention, or can you in all integrity say it is Christ's kingdom that you are seeking to build?

A way to seek God's kingdom is through evangelism by "bringing men from darkness to light and from the power of Satan to God." Are you actively involved in evangelism? How many nonChristians do you know who would consider you a close friend?

Thy will be done. Again notice the Lord Jesus did not say, "My will be done," but "Thy will be done."

This is the same thought that Jesus communicated when He said, "I can of mine own self do nothing: as I hear, I judge: and my judgment is just; because I seek not mine own will, but the will of the Father which hath sent me" (John 6:30).

You cannot pray, "Thy will be done," unless you are actively involved in finding the will of God for your life and doing it. Begin by doing what you know through the Scriptures to be the will of God. If you do this, the Holy Spirit will be faithful to make clear those areas that are uncertain.

Give us this day our daily bread. We can truly pray this prayer only if our attitude is: "All I have comes from and belongs to Jesus." Otherwise, why ask Him for something that "naturally comes to us anyhow"? Paul put it this way: "What? know ye not that your body is the temple of the Holy Ghost *which is* in you, which ye have of God, and ye are not your own? For ye are bought with a price: therefore glorify God in your body, and in your spirit, which are God's" (1 Cor. 6:19-20).

Because Jesus bought you at the price of His blood, you are not your own. You belong to Him. Lordship means recognizing this fact and surrendering all that you are and have and hope to be to Him.

Think over the things that you own which you consider to be precious. It might be your favorite crystal or china, or it may be your sports equipment. Maybe it is your stereo or your automobile. Whatever it is, ask yourself who owns it. If it truly belongs to the Lord Jesus Christ, then of course you will not mind making it available to Jesus to be used as He sees fit.

And forgive us our debts, as we forgive our debtors. Jesus is telling us to pray, "Lord, I want You to forgive me in just the same way that I forgive other people." Could you say that? Could you settle for God forgiving you in proportion to how you forgive others?

Lordship leads to a mutual commitment, involving not only receiving, but giving. *Grace* is God's willingness to commit Himself totally to us. *Lordship* is our willingness to commit ourselves totally to God. Everybody wants God to commit Himself totally to him, but few are willing to commit themselves totally to God.

And lead us not into temptation. Here Jesus is praying that the Father will not lead us into situations where we can be tempted. There are many situations in life that are not wrong in themselves, but they provide opportunities for Satan to overpower us.

Jesus did not say, "Lead us not into *sin.*" He said, "Lead us not into *temptation.*" To pray this prayer means that I am willing to surrender questionable things. I am not only willing to surrender those things that are sin, but I am also willing to surrender all those areas of my life that tend to lead me into temptation.

You yourself know what these areas are. To make Jesus Christ Lord of your life means that you are willing to lay them aside.

Deliver us from [the] evil [one]. This is the same prayer that the Lord Jesus offered for His disciples on the night of His betrayal (see John 17:15).

Lordship involves the recognition that there is no way we can fight our own battles. Christ, and He alone, must keep us. No one in his own strength can do battle with the enemy and win. Even Jesus Christ defeated Satan only at the price of the cross.

James, the brother of our Lord Jesus, puts it this way: "Submit yourselves therefore to God. Resist the devil, and he will flee from you" (James 4:7). The devil will flee from us if we do two things:

first, *submit* ourselves to the Lord, and second, *resist* him in the Lord's strength.

Why Does Jesus Want to Be Our Lord?

Why does Christ bother to get involved in our lives? Why does He not just leave us in our misery? This is one of the great mysteries of the Bible. But the Scriptures are very clear that He loves us and does want to get involved. He does want to be Lord of our lives. When I look at my own sinfulness, my own propensity for evil, I must confess that this is a staggering thought.

I know a salesman from Oklahoma City who uses a small aircraft for business trips because he travels to many out-of-the-way spots across the country. He was flying once over some rugged terrain when he saw an automobile trying to pass a large truck. It was obvious that the driver of the car was extremely impatient to get around the truck; his car crossed back and forth from one lane to the other.

My friend decided to throttle back and watch. Each time the auto sought to pass the truck, it would either reach a double line, a hill, or a bend, or meet another car coming from the opposite direction. From my friend's perspective, he could see several miles down the highway, and he thought, *If I could enter into communication with that man in the automobile, I could tell him when it was safe to pass and when it was unsafe.*

As we are on the move in this great adventure called life, we cannot see around the bend into tomorrow or over the hill into next week. Consequently, we are not sure when it is safe to pass. Because

Jesus Christ is Lord of all, seeing the end from the beginning, He does know.

His willingness to be our Lord reveals His desire to get involved in our lives so He can tell us when it is safe to move ahead and when it is best not to move. Would we not be extremely foolish to turn down such a gracious offer?

Chapter 3

THE COST OF DISCIPLESHIP

Several months ago, a businessman and I were having lunch together. During the meal, I asked him what was uppermost in his thinking. He replied that he was in the process of reevaluating the cost/results ratio in his corporation. The concept was simple. To stay in business, he had to make sure that the cost of manufacturing his product was not greater than the price for which he could sell it.

Even I could understand the importance of a cost/results ratio. If it cost me $5 to make a product, and I sold it for $4.50, I would soon be out of business. As I mused over this concept, I thought how much the benefits of being a Christian exceed the cost. In fact, discipleship has been designed by God, with our best interests at heart. It was not designed to help God out, but rather to help us out.

God does not need our help; we need His. Discipleship was designed by God to give us the help we need.

One spring a family of five was driving through Georgia in a Volkswagen®. It was late at night and raining so heavily they could hardly see 100 feet down the road. As they were inching their way along, they noticed a man and woman walking along the highway in the pouring rain. They pulled over, asked if they could help, and noticed that the woman carried a baby in her arms.

She said they lived in a town several miles back, but the electrical storm had caused a short in the wiring of their house, starting a fire that burned it to the ground. They had barely escaped with their lives and were walking to the next town some seven miles away to stay with her sister and family until further provision could be made. Feeling sorry for the destitute family and realizing there was no room for them in the VW®, the man reached into his wallet, pulled out $20, gave it to the woman, and drove off into the night.

A couple of miles down the highway, he stopped the car and asked his family, "How much money do you have?" Their pooled resources came to a little under $100. He drove back to where the couple was still walking. "Do you have the money I gave you?" he asked.

Quite surprised, the woman said, "Yes, we do."

"Then give it to me."

Perplexed, she reached into her pocket, pulled out the $20 and handed it to him. He combined it with the money he had and handed it all to her saying, "Here, our family would like you to have this."

When I first heard this story, I thought, *What a beautiful and precise illustration of how God treats us.* Our Lord gives us so many wonderful gifts, and then He comes to us and says, "I would like to have them all back—every one of them." He does this so He can combine them with His unlimited resources and give them all to us.

Discipleship is our opportunity to tap the infinite resources of God. It is our chance to give our lives to significance rather than mediocrity. In discipleship we are not doing God a favor. He is doing us a favor. It is vital that the disciple grasp this important concept.

However, Jesus also warns us to weigh the cost and weigh it well, for discipleship will cost us something. It will cost us our lives. But the results are infinitely greater than the cost, so much greater that one would be foolish to turn down such an offer.

Let's walk through Luke 14 together and note some principles of discipleship as Jesus brings this great concept into focus.

Verse 1:

> And it came to pass, as he went into the house of one of the chief Pharisees to eat bread on the sabbath day, that they watched him.

Wherever Jesus went, the eyes of people were upon Him. He claimed to be different. He claimed to be the Author of a brand new way of life. He said, "I am come that they might have life, and that they might have *it* more abundantly" (John 10:10). And because of His claim to uniqueness, people watched His every move to see if He was genuine.

What was true for the Savior in this respect is true for all godly people. The Christian or "Christ-one" is an ambassador of Jesus

Christ. As His disciples, we claim to be in touch with reality; and consequently, the world watches us also.

Our Lord always lived by principle, never by circumstance. As His disciples, how do we live? By circumstance or by principle?

Your car is old; parts are wearing out and are starting to give you trouble. The time has come for you to trade it in. So you make that familiar trek to the dealer. The salesman looks you in the eye. "Is there anything wrong with it?" You now have the choice to live by principle or by circumstance. Do you tell him the truth or a lie? THE DISCIPLE IS ONE WHO IN EVERY AREA OF HIS LIFE DETERMINES FROM THE BIBLE WHAT IS RIGHT AND LIVES IT CONSISTENTLY rather than allowing circumstances to shape his conduct.

Verse 2:

> And, behold, there was a certain man before him
> which had the dropsy.

Jesus was constantly in touch with the needy. They were always "before him." Seldom, if ever, in our Lord's ministry did a person come for help and get turned down. Jesus seemed to deny the Syrophoenician woman, but even then He ultimately met her need.

Another great principle of discipleship comes into focus for us. THE DISCIPLE IS ONE WHO IS IN CONSTANT TOUCH WITH PEOPLE IN NEED. AS Jesus disciple, are you constantly meeting other people's needs?

Verses 8-10:

> "When you are invited by someone to a wedding
> feast, do not take the place of honor, lest someone
> more distinguished than you may have been invited
> by him, and he who invited you both shall come
> and say to you, 'Give place to this man,' and then
> in disgrace you proceed to occupy the last place.
> But when you are invited, go and recline at the
> last place, so that when the one who has invited
> you comes, he may say to you, 'Friend, move up
> higher'; then you will have honor in the sight of all
> who are at the table with you." (NASB)

Jesus is in the house of one of the chief Pharisees. It is time to
eat, and people begin to elbow their way to the best seats around the
table. Observing this, He uses the situation to teach a principle.

When you come to the table, don't take the seat of honor. For
when the host comes in with the guest of honor, he will have to ask
you to move. The host will feel embarrassed because he has to move
you; the guest of honor will feel embarrassed because he has to take
your place; all the other guests will be embarrassed because they have
to witness all this; and you will be embarrassed because you are the
one moved.

Rather, says Jesus, when you come to the table, find the lowest
seat and sit there. Then when the host comes in and realizes that you,
the guest of honor, are sitting in the lowest seat, he will move you to
the seat of honor. As he moves you, he will think, *My, what a humble*

man he is. And as you move from the lowest to the best seat, you will be honored before everyone. How pleasant! Jesus is providing instruction that will result in your feeling good rather than bad.

An important lesson for the disciple emerges from these three verses: namely, that THE COMMANDMENTS OF GOD ARE NEVER WHIMSICAL OR ARBITRARY BUT ARE DESIGNED FOR OUR BEST. God is not in heaven thinking, *I wonder how I can make life miserable for these creatures of Mine.* Instead, He is thinking, *What are some guidelines I can give My children to teach them how to live life to the fullest?* God's laws and commandments are designed to help us, not hinder us. They are meant to make us happy and fulfilled. They were written to keep us out of trouble. If the disciple could learn this one lesson, many of life's problems would be resolved.

Verse 11:

> For whosoever exalteth himself shall be abased; and
> he that humbleth himself shall be exalted.

Just as football has its double reverse, so also does God. It is in the form of a simple truth: our appetites and innate desires are not wrong in themselves but are God-created. They become wrong when we seek to satisfy or fulfill them in an unscriptural way.

For example, there is nothing wrong with wanting to be exalted or to be first or to live or to be free or to be a leader—or any one of a dozen other drives or appetites. What Jesus is saying is that they must be satisfied in His way. The key to being first is being last. The key to living is dying. The key to being free is being Christ's slave. The key to getting is giving. The key to being a leader is being a servant. The key to being exalted is to live a life characterized by humility.

Everybody wants to live, but nobody wants to die. Everybody wants to be free, but nobody wants to be a slave. Everybody wants to get, but nobody wants to give. And this is precisely where we run into conflict with God.

He created the world; He made us; He made life; He made the rules by which we ought to live our lives. So often we want the results that God promises, but we don't want to pay the price. And in our scheming little minds, we think, *Surely it must be possible to get without giving, to be first without really being last, to live without really dying.* And so we endeavor to shortcut God's rules for the game of life. But the Bible teaches us that when we shortcut the rules we short-circuit the system. IN NO WAY CAN A PERSON GET WITHOUT GIVING OR TRULY LIVE WITHOUT DYING. The disciple is one who has learned this great truth and is living his life accordingly.

Verses 15-24:

> And when one of them that sat at meat with him heard these things, he said unto him, Blessed *is* he that shall eat bread in the kingdom of God. Then said he unto him, A certain man made a great supper, and bade [invited] many: And sent his servant at suppertime to say to them that were bidden, Come; for all things are now ready. And they all

with one *consent* began to make excuse. The first said unto him, I have bought a piece of ground, and I must needs go and see it: I pray thee have me excused. And another said, I have bought five yoke of oxen, and I go to prove them: I pray thee have me excused. And another said, I have married a wife, and therefore I cannot come. So that servant came, and shewed his lord these things. Then the master of the house being angry said to his servant, Go out quickly into the streets and lanes of the city, and bring in hither the poor, and the maimed, and the halt, and the blind. And the servant said, Lord, it is done as thou hast commanded, and yet there is room. And the lord said unto the servant, Go out into the highways and hedges, and compel *them* to come in, that my house may be filled. For I say unto you, That none of those men which were bidden shall taste of my supper.

As Jesus is eating with the chief Pharisee and his guests, one of the people in a burst of enthusiasm says, "Blessed is he that shall eat bread in the kingdom of God!" Jesus then proceeds to tell the Parable of the Great Supper. The parable obviously refers to the kingdom of heaven and to that great feast with God the Father and the Lord Jesus Christ. Why would anyone reject an invitation to dine at God's table? Only if they did not know who was extending the invitation. As Paul says, "None of the princes of this world knew: for had they known *it,* they would not have crucified the Lord of glory" (1 Cor.

2:8). The Romans and the religious leaders of the Jews crucified Jesus Christ because they did not know who He was. People today refuse God because they are not aware of who is extending the invitation.

The Parable of the Great Supper reveals that a preoccupation with the insignificant makes it impossible to bring priorities into perspective.

Possibly if our Lord Jesus were to tell the parable today, He would talk about building a dream house instead of buying a piece of ground. Instead of five yoke of oxen, He would refer to a business venture or playing the stock market. His marriage example would remain the same, for marriage through the centuries has never changed.

Becoming a Christian is free of charge. It costs the believer absolutely nothing. "For by grace are ye saved through faith, and that not of yourselves: it is the gift of God: Not of works, lest any man should boast" (Eph. 2:8-9). But there is a cost attached to becoming a disciple. The cost is to become involved in God's "thing" rather than our own. How easy it is for the Christian to become preoccupied with his dreams, his aspirations, his own little deal, and miss God's perfect plan for his life.

Rarely does the Spirit of God shout at a person. His voice usually comes in the form of an inner prodding (as the believer reads the Scriptures). THE DISCIPLE IS ONE WHO IS IN TUNE WITH THE VOICE OF THE SPIRIT OF GOD.

Verse 25:

And there went great multitudes with him.

It has always been in vogue to speak a good word for Jesus. The politician is assured of extra votes if he can work a quote or two from the Bible into his orations. Gandhi, though a staunch Hindu, was an admirer of Jesus Christ. Yes, the multitudes have always followed Jesus. But note who it is that hears Jesus Christ. "Then drew near unto him all the publicans and sinners for to hear him" (Luke 15:1). The multitudes followed Him; the publicans and sinners heard Him.

This is the way it has always been, and it is the way it will probably always be. Christianity is a religion of rescue. It is designed for the desperate. It is for people who have a craving for something more than they can eke out of life by themselves. They are candidates for what Jesus has to say. They are the ones who "hear him," who not only listen to what He says, but act on it. ONE OF THE FUNDAMENTAL REQUISITES FOR TRUE DISCIPLESHIP IS A SPIRIT OF DESPERATION THAT BURNS DEEP WITHIN THE SOUL.

Verses 26-33:

> If any *man* come to me, and hate not his father, and mother, and wife, and children, and brethren, and sisters, yea, and his own life also, he cannot be my disciple. And whosoever doth not bear his cross, and come after me, cannot be my disciple. For which of you, intending to build a tower, sitteth not down first, and counteth the cost, whether he have *sufficient* to finish *it?* Lest haply [otherwise], after he hath laid the foundation, and is not able

to finish *it,* all that behold *it* begin to mock him,
Saying, This man began to build, and was not able
to finish. Or what king, going to make war against
another king, sitteth not down first, and consulteth
whether he be able with ten thousand to meet him
that cometh against him with twenty thousand? Or
else, while the other is yet a great way off, he send-
eth an ambassage, and desireth conditions of peace.
So likewise, whosoever he be of you that forsaketh
not all that he hath, he cannot be my disciple.

Now we begin to talk about the cost. It starts with a willingness
to renounce all other loyalties in preference to Jesus Christ.

Numbers 14 describes the Children of Israel at Kadeshbarnea
about to enter the Promised Land when the twelve scouts return,
bringing back an "evil report." The cost of entering the Promised
Land is far too high; for alas, giants live there, the sons of Anak
(see Num. 13:32-33). In a moment of terror, the people decide to
turn back, with the excuse that the giants would kill their wives and
children.

God never promised there would be no giants. He simply promised that He would assume responsibility for their safe arrival in the
Promised Land. But in their panic, the Hebrews hid behind their
wives and children. One of the first signs of unbelief is an undue
concern for the family.

To be a disciple of Jesus Christ, I must follow Him and do His
bidding even when it appears that it will cost me my mother and my
father, my wife (or husband), my children.

To drive home the impact of this cost, Jesus uses two graphic illustrations—building a tower and preparing for battle.

Verse 28 describes a man starting to build a tower but not finishing it. Have you ever started something and failed to finish it? Have you ever made a promise and failed to keep it? Have you ever vowed a vow and not fulfilled it? If so, Solomon has a word of counsel for you:

> Be not rash with thy mouth, and let not thine heart be hasty to utter any thing before God: for God is in heaven, and thou upon earth: therefore let thy words be few. ... When thou vowest a vow unto God, defer not to pay it; for he hath no pleasure in fools: pay that which thou hast vowed. Better is it that thou should not vow, than that thou shouldest vow and not pay. (Eccl. 5:2, 4–5)

When I lived in Fort Worth I had to make frequent business trips to Dallas. As I drove along the freeway, I used to pass a large structure which appeared to be an unfinished apartment house. The skeleton was there; but for some reason, it was never completed. Month after month I drove past the structure, but there was no apparent progress on the building. Later I discovered that a man had started building, but had miscalculated the cost. He had exhausted his credit and was unable to draw any income from the apartment house. It stood as a monument to his poor planning.

JESUS USED THIS KIND OF SITUATION TO EMPHASIZE THE IMPORTANCE OF COUNTING THE COST OF BEING

A DISCIPLE BEFORE COMMITTING ONESELF. Don't start something unless you are willing to finish it.

Note that Jesus said, "And is not *able* to finish it." The Dallas contractor was *not able* to finish his building. For the disciple, however, the ability traces back to the will. The ability to be a disciple is ours through the resources of Jesus Christ (2 Peter 1:3); the only factor we need to add to the equation is that of our wills.

The Lord Jesus gave a second illustration on counting the cost: a king going to war. When engaging our enemy in battle, two questions must be answered. First, can I with my resources beat him? Second, do I want to pay the price involved in beating him? If the answer to either of these questions is no, it is wiser to send an ambassador and sue for peace.

The Lord Jesus said, "Upon this rock I will build my church; and the gates of hell shall not prevail against it" (Matt. 16:18). Gates are for defense, not offense. Have you ever heard of a person going to battle swinging a pair of gates at the enemy? Gates are used to keep the enemy out. The disciple is called upon to do battle against the massed forces of Satan, to break down the gates of hell and set the prisoners free in Jesus' name. Jesus promises that when we do battle like this, the gates of hell shall not prevail against us. But there is a cost involved in doing battle.

"If you are unwilling to pay the cost," says the Lord, "then send your ambassador and sue for peace." As a Christian you can go to the devil and say, "Look, Satan, I am already a Christian and I am on my way to heaven; but I want to make a deal with you. If you leave me alone, I will leave you alone. I will not be a true disciple of Jesus Christ. I will not threaten your hold over the lives of men or

May it never be

invade your kingdom. In return, don't you bother me. Let me live in comfort and quiet."

And the devil will say, "Friend, you've got yourself a deal."

But remember, Satan is a liar and the father of lies. You have no guarantee that he will not double-cross you. The cost you will pay for not being a disciple is infinitely greater than the cost you will pay for being one.

Verses 34-35:

> "Salt is good; but if even salt has become tasteless,
> with what will it be seasoned? It is useless either for
> the soil or for the manure pile; it is thrown out. He
> who has ears to hear, let him hear." (NASB)

Jesus concludes His dissertation on discipleship with this strange Parable of the Savorless Salt. For a long while, I could not understand its relation to discipleship. Then one day it occurred to me that this parable is an illustration of the believer who refuses to be a disciple. It is God's design that every believer be a disciple. But when one goes back on his commitment, he becomes good for nothing. You can't save him; he is already saved. You can't use him; he is unavailable. He is like savorless salt. Men throw it out.

Week after week as you see him going along to church, he becomes an example of what not to be. All you can say to your "Timothy" is, "See that man? He is a believer who has refused to pay the price of becoming a disciple. In making that decision, he has relegated himself to a life of mediocrity. To use the words of the Lord Jesus, he is savorless salt. Whatever you do, don't become like him."

When Cortez landed at Vera Cruz in 1519 to begin his dramatic conquest of Mexico with a pocket-sized force of 700 men, he purposely set fire to his fleet of eleven ships. His men on the shore watched their only means of retreat sinking to the bottom of the Gulf of Mexico. With no means of retreat, there was only one direction in which to move forward into the Mexican interior to meet whatever might come their way.

IN PAYING THE PRICE FOR BEING CHRIST'S DISCIPLE, YOU TOO MUST PURPOSEFULLY DESTROY ALL AVENUES OF RETREAT. Resolve in your heart today that whatever the price for being His follower, you are willing to pay it. Either that, or send your ambassador and sue for peace.

Chapter 4

A PROPER VIEW OF GOD AND MAN

Every problem a person has is related to his concept of God. If you have a big God, you have small problems. If you have a small God, you have big problems. It is as simple as that. When your God is big, then every seeming problem becomes an opportunity. When your God is small, every problem becomes an obstacle.

Every disciple should have a clear understanding of:

1. Who God is
2. Who he is

You will never have a proper understanding of who God is until you understand yourself. The converse, however is also true. You will never have a true understanding of yourself until you understand who God is. These two ideas are mutually dependent. The two questions of who God is and who we are find answers in Isaiah 40-66. Let's consider some passages.

The Nature and Character of God

Isaiah 40:3-5:

> The voice of him that crieth in the wilderness, Prepare ye the way of the LORD, make straight in the desert a highway for our God. Every valley shall be exalted, and every mountain and hill shall be made low: and the crooked shall be made straight, and the rough places plain: and the glory of the LORD shall be revealed, and all flesh shall see *it* together: for the mouth of the LORD has spoken *it*.

The Bible teaches that God is a glorious, self-manifesting God. The whole purpose of the devotional life is to see His majesty and become absorbed with His glory. We read in verse 4 that God has removed every obstacle standing in the way of our fellowshipping with Him. We see, then, that the Lord is the initiator of the relationship. For us to know God is His idea, not ours. Christianity is unique among the religions of the world in that it consists not of men seeking God, but God seeking men.

Isaiah 40:10-11:

> Behold, the Lord GOD will come with strong *hand,* and his arm shall rule for him: behold, his reward *is* with him, and his work before him. He shall feed his flock like a shepherd: he shall gather the lambs with his arm, and carry *them* in his bosom, *and* shall gently lead those that are with young.

Notice the delicate balance between God's strength and power on the one hand, and His extreme gentleness on the other. Our God is a powerful God, for by Him were all things created (see Isaiah 40:26, 28). The psalmist says, "By the word of the LORD were the heavens made; and all the host of them by the breath of his mouth" (Ps. 33:6). Science has taught us that energy is the substance from which matter is made. God created the universe by the sheer power of His Word. His Word is creative energy.

The illustration in Isaiah 40:11 is that of a shepherd tending his flock. It teaches us that the Lord will do two things—feed us and lead us. He has made all of our needs His responsibility. So also is the burden for giving us His direction.

Isaiah 40:13-14:

> Who hath directed the Spirit of the LORD, or *being* his counsellor hath taught him? With whom took he counsel, and *who* instructed him, and taught him

in the path of judgment, and taught him knowledge, and shewed to him the way of understanding?

These questions are rhetorical, the answer obviously being no one. Why is it that no one has ever been a counselor to God? Or that no one has ever shown Him the way to go? Simply stated, it is that He has never had to ask. He Himself said, "*I am* God, and *there is* none else; *I am* God, and *there* is none like me, declaring the end from the beginning, and from ancient times *the things* that are not *yet* done, saying, My counsel shall stand, and I will do all my pleasure" (Isa. 46:9-10).

Isaiah 40:15-17:

> Behold, the nations *are* as a drop of a bucket, and are counted as the small dust of the balance: behold, he taketh up the isles as a very little thing. And Lebanon *is* not sufficient to burn, nor the beasts thereof sufficient for a burnt offering. All nations before him *are* as nothing; and they are counted to him less than nothing, and vanity.

This puts the world in its proper perspective. It is easy to look at the wrong things and become discouraged—the decadence of the human race, our own propensity for evil, our inability to control ourselves, the fact that our increased technology has often only added to our problems—all of these are enough to make many people cynical and bitter. If it is not war, then it is crime. If it is not crime, then it is scandal. If it is not scandal, then it is natural disasters. Something is always wrong.

World powers do not shape the destinies of men; neither do the economic, political, or philosophical leaders of the world. God says that the mightiest of nations is less than a drop in the bucket, and as insignificant as a tiny speck of dust on a balance. He is in control!

Isaiah 40:28:

> Hast thou not known? hast thou not heard, *that* the everlasting God, the LORD, the Creator of the ends of the earth, fainteth not, neither is weary? *there* is no searching of his understanding.

The Lord God never grows tired, never runs out of ideas, never at a loss as to what to do or where to go. He is in perfect and absolute control. He never makes mistakes. If we would believe this, a lot of our problems in life would be solved.

There are only two persons who can hurt you—you and God. Satan cannot hurt you. This fact comes through clearly in the Book of Job. We read of the conversation between Satan and God (see Job 1), in which Satan says that he cannot touch Job because God has built a "hedge" around him. This is true for every believer. The devil cannot touch him except by divine permission.

The wonderful message of the Bible is that God has our best interests at heart. He does not want to hurt us. He thinks only good thoughts about us. He desires the very best for each one of us. So God has restricted Himself in that He cannot hurt us because of the promises He has made to us.

This, therefore, narrows the field. The only person who can ruin your life is you—no one else. Certainly other people cannot hurt you except with divine permission. If this were not so, it would mean that God is not in control of the destinies of His people. We would then have the ridiculous situation of picturing God wringing His hands in heaven saying, "I sure hope that My servant does not get hit by an automobile or killed in a plane crash."

No one can touch your life but you, and the Bible does teach that it is possible for a person to ruin himself. You are your own worst enemy. But if you are walking by faith and in obedience, and God is who He says He is, then no one else can ruin your life; no one else can make you miss the perfect will of God.

Isaiah 42:1–4:

> Behold my servant, whom I uphold; mine elect, *in whom* my soul delighteth; I have put my spirit upon him: he shall bring forth judgment to the Gentiles. He shall not cry nor lift up, nor cause his voice to be heard in the street. A bruised reed shall He not break, and the smoking flax shall he not quench: he shall bring forth judgment unto truth. He shall not fail nor be discouraged, till he have set judgment in the earth: and the isles shall wait for his law.

This passage is a prophecy relating to Jesus Christ. Jesus said that judgment belongs to Him (see John 5:22-23). The judgment He exercises is according to truth, and it is absolutely consistent with

Himself. We have already seen that He never becomes discouraged or fainthearted over the iniquity of the world. Our God will bring forth judgment and equality to this planet called Earth.

Isaiah 42:8:

> I *am* the LORD: that *is* my name: and my glory will
> I not give to another, neither my praise to graven
> images.

The Lord reminds us again and again that He will share His glory with no one. Paul made the same point when he wrote that there are not very many wise and noble people in the kingdom of God (see 1 Cor. 1:26-29). Instead, God gives wisdom to the base and the despised when it is to be used for God's glory.

The Jewish religious leaders called Peter and John unlearned and ignorant men (see Acts 4:13), and yet these unlearned, ignorant fishermen wrote seven of the New Testament books. These seven books are so profound that, through the centuries, great minds have not been able to fathom their depths.

Isaiah 43:11–18:

> I, *even* I, *am* the LORD; and beside Me *there is* no
> saviour. I have declared, and have saved, and I have
> shewed, when *there was* no strange *god* among you:
> therefore ye *are* my witnesses ... that I *am* God.
> Yea, before the day *was* I *am* he; and there is none

that can deliver out of my hand: I will work, and who shall let [hinder] it?

The Bible teaches that God is man's Savior. He and He alone can save. Consequently, He alone is our security. What He is saying here is: Beside Me there is no security. Our government through its welfare programs seeks to give its citizens security. Corporations promise employees security through pension plans, medical programs, increased wages, better jobs, and stock options. We are told that man can create his own vehicles of security. In reality, only God can save, only God can deliver, only God can redeem. Only God can give man true security.

We have hardly scratched the surface of these great closing chapters of Isaiah regarding the character and nature of God. How easy it is to see when we are able to grasp a vision of His greatness—that all of our problems and anxieties are rather insignificant.

The Nature and Character of Man

Isaiah 40:6-7:

> The voice said, Cry. And he said, What shall I cry? All flesh *is* grass, and all the goodliness thereof *is* as the flower of the field: The grass withereth, the flower fadeth: because the spirit of the LORD bloweth upon it: surely the people *is* grass.

This is how God and the Scriptures view man—not as the great, self-sufficient maker of his own destiny but similar to the grass of the fields—here today, gone tomorrow. James, the brother of the Lord Jesus, put it this way: "For what *is* your life? It is even a vapour, that appeareth for a little time, and then vanisheth away" (James 4:14). In order to understand man this is where we must begin.

The brevity of life helps us realize the importance of giving ourselves to the right thing. The psalmist said:

> For he seeth *that* wise men die, likewise the fool and the brutish person perish, and leave their wealth to others. Their inward thought *is, that* their houses *shall continue* for ever, *and* their dwelling places to all generations; they call *their* lands after their own names. Nevertheless man *being* in honour abideth not: he is like the beasts *that* perish. ... Be not thou afraid when one is made rich, when the glory of his house is increased; For when he dieth he shall carry nothing away: his glory shall not descend after him. (Ps 49:10-12, 16-17)

What was true in the day of the psalmist is true today. "They call their lands after their own names." The states of Maryland, Louisiana, Pennsylvania, Virginia, and North Carolina all stand as a testimony to this! A man in one of the cities of Michigan had a great deal of wealth. Boulevards, schools, and libraries are named after him because of his philanthropic contributions. Just before his death, he came to the city fathers and told them that he would give to them all of his wealth if they would be willing to name the city after him. Brevity of life causes man to cling to it and to reach out for immortality in whatever form he can find it.

Isaiah 47:8-10:

> "Now, then, hear this, you sensual one who dwells securely, who says in your heart, 'I am, and there is no one besides me. I shall not sit as a widow, nor shall I know loss of children.' But these two things shall come on you suddenly in one day: loss of children and widowhood. They shall come on you in full measure in spite of your many sorceries, in spite of the great power of your spells. And you felt secure in your wickedness and said, 'No one sees me.' Your wisdom and knowledge, they have deluded you; for you have said in your heart, 'I am, and there is no one besides me.'" (NASB)

Because man strives for immortality in the wrong way, he runs contrary to the purposes of God. The subject of this passage is Babylon, but it can be readily applied to all of mankind.

In a famous passage prophesying the coming of Jesus Christ, Isaiah wrote, "All we like sheep have gone astray; we have turned every one to his own way" (53:6). Again, the prophet wrote, "But we are all as an unclean *thing,* and all our righteousnesses *are* as filthy rags; and we all do fade as a leaf; and our iniquities like the wind, have taken us away" (64:6).

A proper perspective of God and man shows us that all of the evil and calamity that fall upon man is a product of his own folly and sinfulness. Conversely, all of the good that falls upon man is a product of God's grace and mercy. The natural man takes issue with this. He, in violent disagreement, would turn this around and say that all of man's achievements, his blessings, and his progress are attributed to his own ingenuity and greatness. However, when calamity and disaster strike, he is quick to blame God.

People who have trouble attributing all that is good to God and all that is evil and wrong to the sinfulness of man understand neither the character of God nor the character of man. Now, we must be quick to remind ourselves that circumstances often enter our lives that are a reflection of God's perfect plan but which we, because of our lack of perspective, interpret to be evil. Take, for instance, the cross of Calvary. If you and I had been with the disciples on that eventful day, we, like they, would no doubt have seen the Crucifixion as a tragedy. Likewise, if we had been with the women at the tomb on that Sunday morning when they found it empty, we, like they, would have concluded that a further calamity had struck, that somebody had stolen the body.

However, with the perspective of 2,000 years, we view both the Cross and the empty tomb not as calamities but as victories. Often a seemingly adverse circumstance will strike, such as the loss of a loved one, and from our perspective it has all the marks of a tragedy. But from God's perspective, it may very well be the unfolding of a higher and more beautiful plan.

God's Commitment to Man

Much of Isaiah 40—66 is messianic and, by and large, the promises contained in these chapters are either to the Messiah or to the nation of Israel. However, the Holy Spirit promises, "The counsel of the LORD standeth for ever, the thoughts of his heart to all generations" (Ps. 33:11). Just as we can see in these great chapters the nature of God and man, we can also draw some principles and promises for our own lives.

Consider the promise God makes to us in Isaiah 58:10–12:

> And if you give yourself to the hungry, and satisfy the desire of the afflicted, then your light will rise in darkness, and your gloom *will become* like midday. And the LORD will continually guide you, and satisfy your desire in scorched places, and give strength to your bones; and you will be like a watered garden, and like a spring of water whose waters do not fail. And those from among you will rebuild the ancient ruins; you will raise up the age-old foundations; and you will be called the repairer of the breach, the restorer of the streets in which to dwell. (NASB)

Your light will rise in obscurity. The Lord will assume responsibility for guiding you. During the dry periods in your life, the Lord will satisfy your soul. You will have the privilege of becoming the foundation of many generations. But all of this is qualified by an "if." *If* you will give your soul to the hungry and afflicted. *If* you will devote your life to this kind of a goal and objective, God will in turn prosper you beyond your wildest imagination.

This is God's commitment to man. In His love, He saves us through the finished work of Jesus Christ, and then He blesses and prospers us so that, as we take on the character of Jesus Christ, we can effect a change in the lives of other people. All of this in turn spells "purpose" for the believer. This is what disciple-making is all about.

Let me urge you to look further at Isaiah 40-66. Read through these great chapters three separate times. The first time through, write down all you learn about the nature and character of God. In your second reading, write down all you learn about the nature and character of man. The third time through, write down all that you learn about God's commitment to man. This third reading will stagger you. Having learned of His greatness and our tendency to sin, you will see how graciously He has dealt with us.

Chapter 5

EVANGELISM AND THE DISCIPLE

Being a disciple begins with a proper relationship to Jesus Christ and having on your heart what is on His. *Making* disciples begins with evangelism. As one person put it, the objective in the Christian life is to populate heaven and depopulate hell.

In evangelism the Christian's pacesetter is none other than the Lord Jesus Himself. The fourth chapter of John's Gospel provides us with a striking example of Jesus' approach to evangelism.

Picking the Opportunity

Verse 4:

> And he had to pass through Samaria. (NASB)

Verse 9:

> [The woman of Samaria said to Jesus,] The Jews
> have no dealings with the Samaritans.

What Jesus implied by His interest in her was, "I have dealings with the whole world."

Jesus arrived at Jacob's well tired and thirsty (see vv. 6-7). His needs were simple and easy to understand. He needed rest and refreshment. But instead of satisfying Himself, He created out of His need an opportunity to witness.

When I first discovered this truth in John 4, I was smitten in my conscience. Often I use my need as an excuse not to witness. I remember, for example, a conference on the East Coast. In the course of the weekend, I had spoken four or five times and had had personal interviews with dozens of people. I was tired, and I did not want to get involved in another conversation. On my return home, I made sure that I was one of the first people on the plane, chose a window seat, and then quickly put my briefcase on the seat next to me in an attempt to discourage people from sitting there. I allowed my need to become an excuse not to witness.

As Jesus sat resting, He saw a Samaritan woman come to the well to draw some water. She could hardly be considered a "good opportunity." She was a Samaritan. He was a Jew. Jews had no dealings with Samaritans. She was a woman; He was a man. Men do not counsel women. She was immoral; He was righteous. Righteous people just do not associate with the unrighteous. She was an outcast; He was a great Teacher. She had lost her reputation; and He, by His association with her, would stand a good chance of losing His.

One day I was traveling in an old DC3 on one of the commuter airlines. I was already in my seat when a rather portly lady, probably in her sixties, came and sat next to me. She had given an appearance of cheerfulness and friendliness as she made her way to her seat, laughing and joking with others.

When she sat down, I struck up a conversation with her by saying, "My, you are a happy, young lady."

She reached over, put her hand on my arm, and said, "Young man, you have no idea how miserable I really am. I have all the money I will ever need, but my husband is dead, I have no real friends, and have no reason for living."

By her outward show, there was no way I could have guessed that that woman was a prime candidate for the Gospel of Jesus Christ. Yet, there she was, opening her life to me and letting me know in her own way that she was in desperate need of what the Savior had to offer. What appeared to be a poor opportunity to share Christ was in fact an excellent opportunity.

Principles in Evangelism

There are many principles that can be derived from the ministry of our Lord in the area of evangelism. Eight of them from John 4 should draw our attention. Possibly, this will stimulate your own thinking and cause you in your Bible study to come up with still more.

1. Open the opportunity by asking a favor.

"There came a woman of Samaria to draw water. Jesus said to her, 'Give Me a drink'" (v. 7 NASB).

It is part of our human nature to like to have others feel obligated to us because this makes us feel needed and important. By asking her for a drink of water, Jesus made the Samaritan woman feel needed and important. By revealing His need to her, He created a permissive atmosphere in which she could feel free to talk about her own needs.

A university student once met a beautiful coed in his biology class. Many of his buddies had tried to date her and none of them had met with success. He decided on a novel approach. His sports coat was missing a button, so he asked her if she would sew one on for him. She agreed to do this, and he insisted on returning the favor by taking her out on a date.

In making friends with people, there are many things we can do to make them feel important. On the ski slopes or on the golf course you could say to someone, "Say, I noticed you are really proficient at this. I wonder if you could spare a few moments to give me some tips on how to improve my style." A housewife can use the same approach with her neighbor by asking to borrow a recipe or a cup of flour or some other supplies.

2. Tailor the approach to the person.

"Jesus answered and said to her, 'If you knew the gift of God, and who it is who says to you, "Give Me a drink," you would have asked Him, and He would have given you living water'" (v. 10 NASB).

Jesus did two things here that few people can resist—He offered her a gift and aroused her curiosity.

Shortly after I was married, I purchased a cut-glass bowl for my wife's birthday. I brought it home and left it in the trunk of the automobile until it was time to give it to her. That night as we were lying in bed, I mentioned that I had chosen her birthday present and so aroused her curiosity that she could not sleep until I went out to the car and got it for her.

The Lord Jesus was a master at using the right approach for the right person. He did the same thing with Nicodemus, according to John 3. Recognizing that Nicodemus was a religious leader, Jesus' approach to him was theological: "You must be born again."

The great Bible teacher H. Clay Trumbull was riding on a train next to a person who opened a flask and offered him a drink of whiskey. Dr. Trumbull declined the offer. A few minutes later the man repeated the offer, and again Dr. Trumbull turned him down. The third time the offer was made, the man said to Dr. Trumbull, "I bet you think I am a rather evil man doing all this drinking, don't you?"

"No," said Dr. Trumbull. "I was thinking what a generous man you are to keep offering me a drink." That entree was sufficient for Dr. Trumbull to lead the man to Christ before the journey ended.

3. Choose the questions you want to answer and ignore the others.

The woman of Samaria said to Jesus, "The Jews have no dealings with the Samaritans" (v. 9). Jesus chose to ignore her controversial point. The Samaritan woman again brought up a point of controversy, this time pertaining to the place where people ought to worship God (see v. 20). Now she was striking at a critical issue, and Jesus chose to respond.

In evangelism, develop a feel for the important questions and major in them. Generally speaking, these are questions that deal with getting to know God. Jesus geared His conversation to answering her needs rather than getting entangled in peripheral issues.

When you talk to people about Christ, all kinds of questions come up. "If the Bible says you cannot marry your sister, who did Cain marry?" "What will God do with people who have never heard the message of salvation?"

Many times one is not quite sure how critical the issue is to the person. Is it a genuine problem with him, or is he trying to sidestep the real issues? To help determine this, you can counter with, "If you knew the answer to this question, would it make any difference in your relationship with Jesus Christ?" If his answer is no, you might suggest that the real and important questions center around getting to know God in a personal way. If, however, his answer is yes, then do all that you can to reply. If you don't know the answer, be honest, tell him that you don't, and that you will endeavor to get it for him.

4. Strike for the "open nerve" that causes the person to expose his need.

The Samaritan woman began to argue with Jesus about His ability to draw water by Himself from Jacob's well. Jesus countered with the statement, "Go, call your husband and come here" (v. 16 NASB). She replied that she had no husband, and Jesus completely exposed her with the comment, "You have well said, 'I have no husband'; for you have had five husbands; and the one whom you now have is not your husband" (vv. 17-18 NASB).

The Gospel is the Good News that God can change an individual. This Good News is based on the assumption that each person's needs can be met. In evangelism, therefore, one of the first objectives is to get the person to expose his need.

Suppose you are walking down the street and a stranger appears from nowhere, grabs hold of you, and says, "You look sick. Come with me into my office, and I will operate on you and make you feel better." What do you think your response would be? I would probably flee as fast as I could.

We must be careful not to be guilty of the same approach in evangelism. It is probably not the best approach to walk up to a stranger and say something to the effect, "Do you want to be saved?" Rather, concentrate on getting to know the person. Ask probing questions even before you begin to engage him in a conversation about Jesus Christ. Find out what his needs are, what is occupying his thinking.

A few months ago I was talking to a young coed who was returning from home to the university. In the course of our conversation, she happened to mention that she was majoring in sociology. She had her heart set on being a social worker. I asked her why she chose this career, and she said she had a desire to help people. At this point I was able to ask her what she felt were the real needs people faced. This triggered off a deep, spiritual conversation, during which I was able to share the Gospel.

5. Tell the truth even if it hurts.

"You worship that which you do not know; we worship that which we know, for salvation is from the Jews" (v. 22 NASB). This statement by the Lord Jesus, "salvation is from the Jews," was the very thing that turned Samaritans off. Her initial response to such a statement would probably have been, "Well, here is another bigoted Jew who thinks He's got all the answers." Yet Christ's straightforwardness here gave her confidence and trust in His character when He revealed to her that He was the Messiah. If we hedge on things we know to be true, then we convey to our listeners a lack of trust in our own convictions.

Bible-believing Christians sometimes become embarrassed by the way God acts. To that often-asked question, "Why did God destroy whole nations in the Old Testament?" our inward response frequently is, *O Lord, You've got Yourself into trouble again! Let's see if I can dig You out of this one.*

As you witness, you will meet people who will look you right in the eye and ask, "Do men really go to hell if they don't believe in Jesus Christ?" What will you do? Will you tell them what you know to be the truth? Or will you seek to run around it and change the subject?

This does not mean that we are to be tactless or obnoxious as we talk to people about spiritual truths. Kindness, patience, and long-suffering should be the virtues that characterize our lives (see 2 Tim. 2:24-25). But having said this, we must be willing to tell people the truth.

6. Agree with the person as much as possible.

This principle brings into balance principle number 5. The Jews and Samaritans could not get together on the simplest of questions—namely, where God was to be worshiped (vv. 20-24). Agreeing with the woman as much as possible, Jesus said, "Well, you are partly right. The issue is not between Jerusalem and this mountain. God is a Spirit. You worship Him in spirit and in truth."

A buddy of mine was witnessing to a friend who retorted, "I'm a Catholic and you're a Protestant," as though that should terminate the conversation between them.

My friend said, "Well, that's interesting. I have more in common with my Catholic friends than I do with many of my Protestant friends." That simple statement was enough to bridge a potential argument and allow the conversation to continue.

7. *Don't allow the conversation to get off the subject.*

This principle is seen in how the woman responded to the Lord Jesus when He revealed that the man she was now living with was not her husband. She immediately tried to change the subject by getting into a theological argument over where God was to be worshiped. She tried to avoid the moral issue by asking a theological question.

This often happens when one is talking to people about Jesus if the conversation becomes a bit too personal. Instead of facing up to the personal matters, they might counter with, "What about all those people in nonChristian countries who have never heard the message of Jesus Christ?"

In pursuing the real issue, we must lovingly point out that the question is not so much, "What about people who have not heard?" but rather, "What will you do with Jesus Christ now that you have heard?" However, if this is a genuine question that is an obstacle to the person becoming a Christian, then we must do all we can to find the answer for him (see principle number 3).

8. Be sensitive to how the Holy Spirit is working in the person's life.

Jesus did not push the Samaritan woman; He engaged her in conversation and allowed her to ponder the implications of what had been said. As you read through the story, you notice that salvation became her idea, not just His. She ended up truly wanting it. He did not push it on her.

A beautiful illustration of this is found in Acts 2:36-38. Peter had just finished his great sermon at Pentecost. He gave no invitation. He did not tell his audience what to do. He merely ended with a divine claim—Jesus was the Christ. But what he said shook them; and because the Spirit of God was working in their hearts, salvation became their idea, not Peter's. They took the initiative, asking, "Men *and* brethren, what shall we do?"

Peter's reply was, "Repent, and be baptized every one of you in the name of Jesus Christ."

When you talk to people about Christ, you can often tell where they are by their changing view of who He is. This can be seen by the Samaritan woman's response to Christ. First, she calls Him a Jew (v. 9). Next, she addresses Him as Sir (v. 11). Then, she calls Him a prophet (v. 19). Finally, she confesses Him as the Christ (v. 29).

Passion to Do the Job

Jesus said that His food was to do God's will. This is what concerned Him, what was uppermost in His mind. He told His disciples, "My meat is to do the will of him who sent me, and to finish his work. Say not ye, There are yet four months, and *then* cometh harvest?

behold, I say unto you, Lift up your eyes, and look on the fields; for they are white already to harvest" (John 4:34-35). Jesus does not say here that He is exercising His gifts, or that He really loves to talk to people about their eternal destiny. He simply says that He is doing the will of God.

People shun evangelism because they say it is not their strength, it is not their gift, or they do not enjoy doing it. I can certainly empathize with that. Evangelism is engaging the enemy in what the Bible calls "spiritual warfare." It means fighting the forces of darkness for the souls of people. Let's face it, few people enjoy fighting.

A buddy of mine, a marine infantry officer, once confided that he loved to lead men. He enjoyed going out on bivouac and practicing maneuvers with them. He loved the thrill of the dress parade. But when he was in Vietnam engaging the enemy in combat and seeing his own men die, he realized that he hated fighting.

What is true in physical warfare is equally true in spiritual warfare. If you do not enjoy engaging people in spiritual combat, don't feel that you stand alone. Few people enjoy it. That really is not the question, nor is the question one of whether evangelism is your gift or your strength.

The only relevant question is whether it is the will of God—and we know from the Scriptures that the will of God is for us to do the work of evangelism. The disciple's ministry begins with evangelism.

Chapter 6

RECRUITING A
PROSPECTIVE DISCIPLE

There is strong competition today to gain peoples' allegiance. Many civic-minded organizations are attracting people by the score. If it is not the Red Cross or the United Way, then it is the lodge, the Boy Scouts, the women's club, or a thousand and one other committees, programs, and organizations. As if this were not enough, we face the constant secularization of our society with its accompanying materialism. There is the theater, the country club, horse racing, television, football, and a host of other sports.

Nowadays if a young man wants to move up the organizational ladder of a corporation, he has to pledge his total commitment to the company. Eight hours a day, five days a week, and good, hard work are just not enough. Go-ahead corporations want the young man to eat, sleep, and breathe their vision or product.

Into this arena of competition step the bold claims of Jesus Christ. Jesus said, "If any *man* will come after me, let him deny himself, and take up his cross daily, and follow me" (Luke 9:23). Today, as always, Jesus is calling for disciples, not just Sunday Christians. His men and women refuse to yield to the lure of the world's system. In the world, yes; of the world, never. This type of a person has only one Lord—Jesus Christ. He and He alone orders the life; He determines where time, money, and other resources are spent.

As ambassadors of Jesus Christ, we are in the business of recruiting men and women to a life of discipleship. As we do this, there are some basic, though often forgotten, principles that are essential to follow if we are to recruit the kind of people God can use. Earlier, we discussed certain characteristics or qualities that have to be present in a person's life if he is to be usable in God's sight. Here we want to consider things that the recruiter must implement if he is to get quality people involved in God's work. Again, let me remind you that this is in no way an exhaustive list, but is simply meant to stimulate your thinking.

Recruit to a Vision, Not to an Organization.

An organization, however great it may be, is never highest in God's value system. God gives a vision. An organization must serve this vision. It can never be the vision. By organization, I mean any organized work, whether it be a church—Baptist, Methodist, Presbyterian; a Christian organization—Young Life, Youth for Christ, The Navigators, Campus Crusade, InterVarsity; or a group within a church—the men's fellowship, the women's guild, the young people's gathering.

We do not decide to have an organization and then seek to staff it with a president, vice-president, and secretary. On the contrary, we involve ourselves in what we know to be the will of God, and if through that involvement we become numerically prosperous and need to organize, well and good.

The disciple must be careful never to preach faithfulness in order to make his organization more successful. How easy it is to fall into this trap. Our Sunday school attendance begins to lag, so we have a membership drive. From all outward appearances, this is to get people involved in God's work, but more often than not, it has to do with statistics and breaking records rather than majoring on people getting into the Word of God. If we emphasize meeting peoples' spiritual needs, the chances are that membership numbers will take care of themselves.

Jesus said, "And I, if I be lifted up from the earth, will draw all *men* unto me" (John 12:32). John explains in the next verse that this was to signify the type of death the Christ should die. There is, nonetheless, a fundamental truth suggested here when we, in our ministry, exalt the person of Jesus Christ, men will be drawn to Him.

I once had the privilege of observing a church in Upper Michigan. Every year, the pastor, along with the elders, would ask the representatives from each group in the church to defend their right for existence on the basis of two criteria: (1) the legitimacy of their goals and objectives; (2) the degree to which they achieved those goals and objectives.

If any group did not meet both of these criteria, the elders of the church would disband it. What a terrific idea! If we would ruthlessly apply this practice in all of our churches, it would doubtless contribute to a more vital and healthy fellowship.

The women in a local church decide to pray for the missionaries their church is sponsoring. Once a week they gather for that purpose. The first week they meet in Mrs. Jones' house, and Mrs. Jones prepares for them an assortment of cookies and tea and coffee. The next week they are at Mrs. Smith's house, and she, not wanting to be outdone by Mrs. Jones, does a slightly more elaborate job of preparing refreshments. As the weeks become months the food preparation becomes increasingly more prominent. More and more time is spent around the table chatting, and less and less time is spent praying. The original purpose for the women's missionary guild was noble in deed, but their vision, which constituted the reason for their meeting, somehow went out of focus.

On numerous occasions in various dormitories and military barracks, I have confronted young men with the claims of Jesus Christ. Inevitably, when I meet someone and tell him I would like to talk with him about Christ, his reply is, "What denomination are you with?" Have we brainwashed the nonChristian world into believing that we are more interested in recruiting people to our particular denomination than we are to the person of Jesus Christ? It is so easy to fall into the trap of asking people to be faithful to pet programs rather than to the will of God. I learned long ago that those we are trying to recruit can tell the difference between the two.

Do Not Create the Impression that People Are Doing You or God a Favor by Being Faithful to the Cause of Christ.

The apostle John relates an incident that occurred in the ministry of our Lord Jesus. The people wanted to crown Him as their king, but Jesus, sensing that their motives were impure, countered with some honest but hard-hitting observations. John says, "From that *time* many of his disciples went back, and walked no more with him." At this point, Jesus did a rather startling thing. He turned to the twelve and said to them, Will ye also go away? (John 6:66-67)

I do not believe that the Lord Jesus was feeling sorry for Himself. No, our Lord Jesus was once again underlining the cost involved in being His disciple.

If we neglect this important principle, we run the risk of recruiting unfaithful men. Deuteronomy 20:8 records God's prerequisites for the men who were to be involved in battle. "And the officers shall speak further unto the people, and they shall say, What man *is there that is* fearful and fainthearted? let him go and return to his house, lest his brethren's heart faint as well as his heart."

Getting involved with God has always been on a volunteer basis. Irrespective of how great the need—and the need is great—Christ will not sacrifice quality in order to gain quantity. As His ambassadors, neither can we.

One day I was asked to preach in one of the churches in the town where I lived because the pastor was going out of town. As I talked with one of the elders on the phone, I asked if he would like me to teach in the Sunday school as well as preach at the morning worship service. He assured me that this would not be necessary since they had their appointed Sunday school teachers who would do the job.

After the morning service I was standing by the door shaking hands with members of the congregation as they left, when suddenly the Sunday school superintendent bustled up to me. With a rather flustered look on his face, he stuffed some materials into my hand, saying, "Here, I would like you to teach the young adults class; Mr. Griffin is not at church today."

I pointed out to him that I had been assured that it would not be necessary for me to teach Sunday school, and for that reason I was not prepared. Turning to leave, he mumbled, "Well, if you don't teach, no one else will; and besides, I am not that prepared for the lesson I have to take either!"

So there I stood with the Sunday school materials in my hand wondering how it was that such a thing could happen. I pondered it for some time afterward and finally decided that it was probably the result of something that took place months previously when the superintendent was in the process of recruiting teachers. One by one, he would ask people to teach a class, and one by one they would turn him down with a statement to the effect that they did not feel qualified.

Now take the example of Mr. Elliott. He did not really believe that he was unqualified when he gave this excuse. If the superintendent had said, "Mr. Elliott, I realize that you are not a qualified teacher, but are rather incompetent in this field; however, because of our desperate plight, I wonder if you would teach a Sunday school class," Mr. Elliott would have left the church in a rage. No, the excuse he used was his way of saying that he did not want to pay the price of getting involved.

With everyone declining, the superintendent got desperate and began to plead with some of the people. One person eventually condescended, "Well, all right. As a favor to you, I will go ahead and teach." Now I ask you, with this kind of an attitude, what sort of job is he going to do? His preparation will be haphazard and will probably take place during the commercials as he watches his favorite television programs on Saturday night. And if he does not feel like showing up or if he has some other commitments on Sunday, he does not hesitate to be absent.

Our Savior feels honored and privileged to have us committed as His disciples, but God forbid that we should feel that we are doing Him a favor in being faithful. Similarly, if we cannot staff our programs with the right kind of people, then we should seriously think about terminating the programs. I believe that there is one thing worse than not having any program at all, and that is having a program with the wrong type of leadership.

Grow into Business—Don't Go into Business.

This principle teaches us that we should start small and build in depth rather than concentrate on becoming large and, as a result, end up being top-heavy. When you try to go into business rather than grow into business, you spread your resources thin and dissipate your efforts (see Prov. 24:27).

Let's say that you and I decided that we wanted to go deer hunting together and our objective was to bag as many deer as we could.

Early one morning we find ourselves at the edge of a large clearing where 30 to 40 deer are grazing. We have two guns with us, a 30.06 with a telescopic sight and a 20-gauge shotgun.

Excitedly I whisper to you, "Use the shotgun—that way we might hit almost every deer in the clearing."

"But we won't kill any of them that way," you whisper back. "Let's use the 30.06, for then we can at least get one, maybe even two."

"Yes, but if you use the 30.06, all the rest of them will get away."

Here, then, is our dilemma. Do we want the satisfaction of knowing that we hit every deer in the clearing even though it means that all of them will get away? Or, do we want the satisfaction of bringing home one or possibly two deer, knowing that in so doing we left the rest untouched? I am sure that we would be unanimous in our decision to use the 30.06 rather than the shotgun.

Our ministry should have a pulsating rhythm to it of thrust and conserve. First, recruit a small band of individuals and then throttle back and build deeply into their lives. It is only after you have properly discipled them that you should thrust out again into another program of recruitment. Do not seek to involve yourself with more people than you can adequately handle.

Tailor the Job to the Person Rather Than the Person to the Job.

We must be extremely careful not to recruit people to use them. Our goal should be to help them, and people can usually tell the difference.

When the Lord Jesus met the rich, young ruler, He told him to give away his wealth to the poor and then come and follow Him. The Savior was not trying to use the young man by asking him to lend support to the ministry, but rather was trying to meet the man's need—the first step being to divorce himself from his inordinate affection for wealth.

Prayerfully determine what the person you are helping needs and then help him in that area rather than finding out what he can do best and asking him to do that. The time will come when we will want to maximize his gifts and abilities, but in the initial stages of the discipling process, we must major in his needs. Our Lord Jesus is far more interested in what a person is than in what he can do. "It is for you to be—it is for God to do."

Discipleship Must Take into Consideration the Development of the Whole Man.

Development implies training. Someone might well say, "I thought we were discussing recruitment at this point, not training." We are, but we must remember that in the Christian life, unlike other pursuits, recruitment and training go hand in hand. Let me illustrate.

When a young man is recruited into the marine corps, the first person he meets is a very polite, friendly officer who expounds to him all the virtues and advantages of the corps. After the recruit has signed on the dotted line, he is sent to boot camp, and there he meets the meanest, ugliest, most unpleasant man on the face of the earth—his drill instructor. The recruit's initial reaction is, *What in the world have I gotten myself into?* But by then it is too late. There

is absolutely nothing the recruit can do about it. The drill instructor could not care less how the recruit feels about him, the training
process, or the marine corps in general. He is involved in training
only, not recruitment.

This is not so in the Christian life. The Bible teaches that our
involvement in Christ's army is strictly on a volunteer basis—a person
can leave anytime he wants. Recruitment, therefore, to discipleship
must continue during the training process. We continue to recruit
the would-be disciple to Christ by showing him that we are seeking
to help him develop in every area of his life.

For the sake of simplicity, let me suggest that development can
be categorized into three areas: teaching, training, and building. I
will define *teaching* as the imparting of knowledge, *training* as the
imparting of skill, and *building* as the imparting of character. The
development of our disciple must include all three: teaching, training, and building.

Suppose we want to teach our disciple to do evangelism. We sit
him down and show him the various techniques, such as the ones we
saw in Jesus' encounter with the Samaritan woman. He learns how
to open a conversation about Christ. He memorizes key verses on
the various aspects of the Gospel. He may even master two or three
illustrations that can be used when witnessing to someone. Having
taught him these things, is our job now accomplished? No, for he has
never gone out and talked to anyone about Christ.

So now we need to train him. As the two of us go out to do
evangelism together, both of us are fearful, he more than I, so I
promise that I will begin the conversation; all he needs to do is
observe. We do this a number of times until gradually I begin to

involve him in the conversation with me. As he becomes increasingly more comfortable and proficient, he takes more and more of the conversation himself. Finally he is doing all the talking, and I am only observing. He can now lead a person to Christ as well as I can—maybe better. Is my job of imparting evangelism to him now finished? No, not yet.

Suppose that after all this your disciple has no heart for evangelism. Suppose that in his theology he believes that God will save whom He will save and will let perish whom He will let perish; and that, since in the final analysis evangelism is God's work, not man's, there is no need to get involved in evangelism. If this is the case, then he will cease to evangelize the day we part company.

One final factor is necessary for his development—the building process. Here we seek to change the disciple's sense of values, and thereby ultimately to affect his whole personality. You can see that the farther we go in the development process, the more difficult the task becomes Building is far more difficult than either teaching or training How do you build into a person's life? How do you go about influencing personality? Here are some suggestions:

- Do a Bible study on a character trait that is lacking in his life. Help him see God's perspective on the matter.
- Create an environment in which the desired character trait is evident. If he stays in an environment in which evangelism is evident, then it is more likely that he will embrace it as a conviction of his own.

- Most important, pray the character trait into his
  life.

Scripture says that Jesus "increased in wisdom and stature, and in favour with God and man" (Luke 2:52) Here we see the four areas of our Savior's development as a young man:

WISDOM—the intellect
STATURE—the physical
IN FAVOR WITH God—the spiritual
IN FAVOR WITH MAN—the social

When we recruit men and women to become disciples of Jesus Christ, we should think of their development in these four areas. This does not mean that we have to be an expert in each of these areas in order to train a disciple. Our job is not to accomplish the whole task but to see that it gets done.

This is where the body of Christ complements you in the disciple-making ministry. Draw on the experience and expertise of a variety of people. As you work with your Timothy, your job is simply to see that he gets all the help and attention that he needs—just as a parent does with his child.

There Must Be a Proper Balance between Love and Rebuke.

There is probably as much said in the Bible about love as about any other single subject. God's disposition toward us is one of love, and He expects our disposition toward others to be the same. You will remember that the Lord Jesus called love one of the marks of discipleship, for He said, "A new commandment I give unto you, That ye love one another; as I have loved you, that ye also love one another. By this shall all *men* know that ye are my disciples, if ye have love one to [for] another" (John 13:34-35).

The Lord did not say that people will know that you are His disciple by the number of verses you memorize, or by the frequency with which you attend church, or by the number of people that you lead to Christ. He says, "By this shall all men know that you are My disciples, if you have love one for another."

But this love must be blended with rebuke. Possibly one of the greatest weaknesses in the body of Christ today is that we have surrendered our responsibility to discipline one another. Solomon in all of his wisdom was directly to the point on this subject when he said, "Open rebuke *is* better than secret love. Faithful *are* the wounds of a friend; but the kisses of an enemy *are* deceitful" (Prov 27:5-6).

A friend once shared with me that his application from studying that passage in Proverbs was to pray that God would cause at least one person each week to rebuke him on some area of his life that needed attention. That's quite a challenge isn't it?

"Reprove not a scorner, lest he hate thee: rebuke a wise man, and he will love thee" (Prov. 9:8). Quite often, the reason people do not rebuke us is that they are afraid of our response. They are afraid we will take it in a negative way, and they do not want to have their friendship or relationship with us jeopardized. So when they see things amiss in our lives and want to help us, they are constrained to keep quiet because they suspect that we are "scorners" rather than "wise men."

When was the last time somebody came up to you and pointed out something wrong in your life? If it has not been for quite awhile, it is certainly not because your life is above reproach. Things need correction in your life just as they do in mine. The only way people will call these areas to our attention is if they realize that we are truly wise people who will recognize that any rebuke they administer is done in love.

People are drawn into discipleship by giant doses of love. But if love is to come across as biblical love, it must be blended with rebuke. The kind of people God can use are those who respond to such a blend; Jesus cannot use people who feel sorry for themselves when corrected.

You Recruit a Person to Discipleship by Being His Servant.

The mark of leadership is servanthood. Chesty Puller, considered by many as "Mr. Marine," stated once that the Marine Corps needed men who could lead, not command. A commander tells people what to do; a leader shows people what to do by personal example.

This is definitely one of the toughest aspects of the discipling process. All of us like to be pampered and waited on, but few of us like to roll up our sleeves and wait on others. Yet, this is precisely how people are recruited to the cause of discipleship. Few things are as impressive as seeing a person voluntarily serve others. Men, when was the last time that you served your wife by helping to do the dishes, or did some other job that needed doing around the home? When was the last time you helped your children by making their beds or by tidying their rooms for them?

All of us who know God's Word like to be called servants, but none of us wants to act like a servant or to be treated like one. We must recognize this tendency, which is based in human pride, and fend against it.

You Reproduce after Your Own Kind Whether You Like It or Not.

This is one of the most sobering truths in the Bible. Many cannot and will not identify with the apostle Paul when he says, "Be ye followers of me." We piously say to ourselves and our disciples, "Paul may have been able to say that, but I certainly could never say that. Don't follow me, follow Jesus Christ." The fact of the matter is your disciple will follow you whether you want him to or not.

When you begin to help a person in the Christian life, he will follow you just as naturally as a young child follows his parents, and more likely than not, he will become what you are, not what you say. I have seen this again and again in the Christian life. The leader may preach repeatedly that people ought to be involved in evangelism, but unless he himself is involved in it, the chances are very remote that his people will be involved. Many illustrations in Scripture bear witness to the fact that you reproduce after your own kind. Abraham passed his wife off as his sister in order to save his own skin (Gen. 20:2). His son Isaac did the same thing (Gen. 26:7). The Bible tells us that Eli, the high priest, did a poor job in raising his sons (1

Sam. 2:12-17). He reproduced this quality in the life of his protégé, Samuel (1 Sam. 8:1-5).

It is imperative, therefore, that you major on being the kind of person you want your disciple to become. You can know for certain that you will reproduce what you are in his life. That is why this book began with the chapter, "The Kind of Person God Uses." In order for these qualities to be in the life of your disciple, they must first be in your life.

If you suspect for a moment that the essential qualities of a disciple are not in your own life, then this is where everything must start for you. Go back to chapter one and begin by implementing qualities of godliness in your own life.

Chapter 7

HOW TO TRAIN A DISCIPLE—FOLLOW-UP

Making disciples begins with the task of evangelism. If we work only with Christians in our disciple-making ministry, then the net gain to the kingdom of God is zero. Aggressive evangelism is the mark of the committed disciple, and it is primarily from the fruit of this evangelism that he chooses his Timothy—the person he seeks to disciple.

If the first step in the disciple-making process is evangelism, then the second is follow-up. It is one thing to engage the enemy in combat and set the captives free, but it is altogether another thing to spend the necessary time with a new convert to see that he grows and matures into the likeness of Jesus Christ. In physical reproduction the responsible parents' task only begins when the child is born. Afterward come years of careful nurture and training to ensure that the child develops to the point where he can marry and assume responsibility for his own family.

Follow-up, then, is spiritual pediatrics—the care and protection of the spiritual infant. It deals with the development of new babes in Christ from the time of their new birth until they grow and provide for themselves.

The Bible teaches us that God has a father's heart. We saw this in our study of Isaiah 40 66. Jesus Himself taught us to refer to God as "our Father." Follow-up then is relating to the young Christian the loving concern that our God has shown toward us. We are shocked to the point of unbelief when we hear of a baby being left alone without proper care, but for some reason, our consciences are dulled when we hear of new babes in Christ being neglected. Left alone, they slip into carnality.

Many are afraid to become involved in the task of follow-up because they feel inadequate. They do not think they know enough about the Christian life to assume the responsibility of becoming a spiritual parent. Or they feel that they have so far to go in the Christian life themselves that someone should be teaching them rather than they teaching someone else. All of these feelings of inadequacy are quite normal and probably will never leave. They merely parallel the human (or physical) situation. I have never met parents who, while raising their children, felt they had all the answers.

Follow-up is nothing more and nothing less than parental concern coupled with common sense. There are, however, some basic guidelines for helping a new Christian reach maturity. What are the responsibilities of parents toward their newborn children? Let us briefly analyze a few of the more obvious ones.

Ensure Proper Care and Deal with Trouble Areas

My oldest child, Deborah Lynn, was born with hyalite membrane disease. A membrane formed around that part of the lung which mixes oxygen with the blood. In most cases, children born with this disease die. Our child was given just a 10 percent chance of survival. You can imagine how grateful we were when we discovered that Deborah had the most eminently qualified pediatrician in the city taking care of her. He immediately put her in isolation and took every precaution to make sure she lived. By God's grace, she did, and today Deborah Lynn is a healthy young woman.

The care and concern the doctor gave Deborah Lynn serves as a beautiful illustration of the diligent involvement required of us when dealing with new Christians. Assuming that you have the responsibility for a new babe in Christ, here are some suggestions:

1. Go over again carefully with him the plan of salvation.

"And this is the record, that God hath given to us eternal life, and this life is in his Son. He that hath the Son has life; *and* he that hath not the Son of God hath not life" (1 John 5:11-12).

Every person who has the Son has life. You can ask the new Christian, "Where is Jesus Christ tonight?" Wherever else this babe says Christ is, he should also say that Christ is in his heart. An illustration of a pencil inside a Bible can be used—the Bible representing Jesus Christ and the pencil, eternal life. If the believer has the Bible (Jesus Christ), then he also has the pencil (eternal life), for eternal life is to be found in the Son.

Unfortunately many Christians spend years of their lives living in a fog of uncertainty. Because they do not understand what the Scriptures teach on the subject, they lack assurance of salvation. Proper growth and development can only stem from the new Christian knowing that he is a child of God for all eternity.

2. Pray for him.

The overwhelming majority of New Testament prayers deal not with the unsaved, but with the growth and maturity of new Christians. Two great prayers of Paul in Ephesians, for example, deal with his concern for their growth and maturity (see Eph. 1:15-23; 3:14-20).

I find that prayer is the hardest work I can engage in as a Christian. At the same time, it is the most important part of follow-up. If you also find that prayer is hard work, let me suggest that you simply pray for your new Christian the same prayers that you find in the Bible, such as those in Ephesians. You can do a study on the New Testament prayers that would be applicable and then use them as part of your follow-up program.

Another thing I do is think through the areas in which I am having difficulty; then intercede for my friend in these matters. The Bible says, "There hath no temptation taken you but such as is common to man" (1 Cor. 10:13). All of us fight the same temptations and have the same basic needs.

3. Visit him soon and frequently after his decision for Christ.

This is particularly important during the days immediately following his conversion experience. Satan regroups and marshals his counteroffensive, and the new Christian is particularly vulnerable because he does not understand the nature of spiritual warfare or the great truths in the Bible that can help him through trials and temptations.

In the first ten days of a child's life, his mother must be with him almost constantly. The older the child becomes, the less frequently she needs to see him. Again, what is true in the physical realm is also true in the spiritual.

One of the most significant ministries you can have with your new Christian is that of encouragement. Let him know that he is now a part of the family of God and that the two of you are brothers in Christ. One of the things that Satan will try to deceive him into believing is that the temptations and problems that he faces are unique to him. Encourage him with the fact that we all fight the same problems; and not only this but during these times of temptation, you want to stand together with him against them.

Ensure a Proper Diet

When little Deborah Lynn finally came home from the hospital, victorious over her disease, we had to bear the responsibility for feeding her regularly. We fed her not when we wanted to but when she wanted to be fed—and often this was at the most inconvenient times. One thing was certain: we did not ask her to manage for herself. It would have been cruel to say to her, "Sweetheart, if you want to eat, there is plenty of food in the refrigerator; help yourself."

The proper spiritual diet for a new Christian should include at least:

1. A consistent quiet time.

In Mark 1:35 we read of one of the habits the Lord Jesus developed. "And in the morning, rising up a great while before day, he went out, and departed into a solitary place, and there prayed." Each day should begin with a brief period of fellowship with the Lord, for thus the believer gets his spiritual nourishment for the day. The quiet time should include a time of prayer and some time in the Word. The simple acrostic ACTS is useful in helping a person get started in prayer.

Adoration—Begin with a time of worship, praying over the greatness of God. Encourage the new Christian to use some of the great prayers in the Bible such as that in 1 Chronicles 29:11-14.

Confession—This is a time of acknowledging our sinfulness and our dependence on the Lord. "If we confess our sins, he is faithful and just to forgive us *our* sins, and to cleanse us from all unrighteousness" (1 John 1:9). This verse is the Christian's bar of soap. Let us imagine that my little child, acting in disobedience, goes outside and plays in the mud. As she comes in crying and asking for forgiveness, not only do I forgive her, but I take her into the bathroom, wash her from head to foot, and wash her clothes so that, when we are through, it is as though she had never been outside. This is the promise the Lord Jesus makes to the believer in 1 John 1:9.

Thanksgiving—The long list of sins mentioned in Romans 1 begins with the phrase in verse 21, "neither were thankful." Early in the Christian life the believer must learn the importance of being thankful. This part of the prayertime consists of enumerating the many blessings bestowed on us by our gracious God. Scripture says, "Every good gift and every perfect gift is from above, and cometh down from the Father of lights, with whom is no variableness, neither shadow of turning" (James 1:17).

Supplication—We spend time praying for others—our family, friends, church, country. You can help the young Christian in this aspect of prayer, teaching him how to use prayer pages. Take a sheet of paper and draw a line down the middle, entitling the left-hand column "Requests" and the right-hand column "Answers." Beside each request list the date entered. When the prayer is answered, jot down how it was answered with the date. In a graphic way, this will show the new Christian the marvelous way that God answers prayer.

Of the many good helps available to the Christian for his quiet time, two favorites of mine are: *The Quiet Time*, published by InterVarsity Press, and *Seven Minutes with God*, published by The Navigators.

Help the young Christian to be consistent in having his quiet time by initially having it with him. For example, have a quiet time with him every morning during the first week of his new walk with the Lord. During the second week, meet with him every other morning, and then once a week for the next month or two.

Encourage him to begin with a short period of time with the Lord rather than with a protracted time. This is the beauty of the little plan mentioned in *Seven Minutes with God*. It is better to have seven minutes with the Lord consistently every day and stay with it, than to begin by having one hour with the Lord every morning, and then quit in discouragement.

2. Bible reading.

"As newborn babes, desire the sincere milk of the word, that ye may grow thereby" (1 Peter 2:2). Start the young Christian with a small portion, preferably from the New Testament or the Psalms and incorporate it in his quiet time.

One method that has worked with a great deal of success is to read a paragraph or two and, as you meditate on it, circle or mark one verse that is particularly meaningful. This becomes the favorite verse for the morning. Do this for six mornings, each morning picking out a favorite verse. Then during the quiet time on the seventh morning, review the six favorite verses, and pick out the one that is the favorite among the favorites. That verse can then be written on a small card and memorized.

3. Bible study.

The most important goal of follow-up is to teach the young Christian how to feed himself from the Word of God. Expose him to mature Christians who can feed him, and thus teach him "the whole counsel of God," but remember this can never be a substitute for the person learning how to feed himself.

I remember in those early days of little Deborah's life what a joy it was to hold her and feed her. There she was, nestled in my arms—two eyes, a nose, and a bottle. As she became older, however, we encouraged her to learn to feed herself. So important was this to us as parents that we did not even mind when she used her fingers to eat. We knew that the process of teaching her how to eat graciously would be slow and arduous. But it was also essential.

In the initial stages of follow-up, you and your pastor will have to do most of the feeding of the new babe. For many new Christians, the task of learning how to feed themselves from the Word of God is laborious. It has a tendency to appear legalistic and unfruitful. For this reason, the new Christian will often be tempted to quit trying. Realizing this temptation, you will have to work closely with him, encouraging him to stay with it.

There are many good Bible-study helps on the market but, unfortunately, there are few that I know of that teach a person how to feed himself. The Navigators have a Bible study series, *Design for Discipleship,* the objective of which is to teach the young Christian what it means to become a disciple and to wean him from Bible-study aids in the process so that eventually he can take the Bible and feed himself without any outside helps other than the Holy Spirit. Another excellent book on how to do Bible study is *Independent Bible Study* by Irving L. Jensen. I would recommend this for the mature Christian. (Editor's note: Also available in this category are *Unlocking the Scriptures* and *Opening the Book* by Hans Finzel.)

Whatever Bible-study method is employed, it should include a period of time when the young Christian prepares the study on his own, and then a period of time when he meets together with a group of people who also have done the study and who share their results and learn from one another. In the early weeks of learning how to do Bible study, you will want to prepare the lesson with the new Christian. There is just no substitute for going through these growth processes step by step.

Ensure Love and Affection

There is one thing it is impossible to give people too much of, and that is love. People misunderstand what love is all about and imagine it to be synonymous with spoiling people. The two are in no way related. Sociologists and psychologists tell us that if a child is deprived of love in the early years of his life, it is questionable whether he will ever be able to understand what it truly means to love and be loved. One of the basic needs in life is to be loved and wanted. We need to apply the principle of TLC (Tender Loving Care) to our babes in Christ. Envelop the young Christian with love!

1. Invite him over to your home for meals and make him feel a part of the family.

Bob Wheeler, a carpenter by trade, was the person who led me to Christ many years ago. One of the most significant things he did was to involve me in his family life. His home was my home. I always felt welcome. I cannot recall how many times I ate at his table, but I know I virtually ate him out of house and home! When I think of Bob, I think of 1 Corinthians 16:15: "Know the house of Stephanas, that it is the firstfruits of Achaia, and *that* they have addicted themselves to the ministry of the saints." It became so meaningful to me that my wife and I adopted it as the verse we would claim for our own home.

2. Involve him in the warmth and fellowship of the church.

The writer of the Book of Hebrews warns, "Not forsaking the assembling of ourselves together, as the manner of some *is*, but exhorting *one another;* and so much the more, as ye see the day approaching" (Heb. 10:25).

There is a certain chemistry that takes place in the fellowship of believers which produces an environment that is conducive to growth and stability. I can remember when Bob took me to church for the first time. His friends became my friends. The fellowship and encouragement they showed me was a major factor in my development as a Christian.

Church was where I had an opportunity to observe other believers and to adopt their lifestyle as mine. There was a great deal in my old life that had to be discarded, and a great deal of new life that had to be incorporated. That small church played a major role in my making that transition.

3. Take him with you.

It is written of the Lord Jesus, "And he ordained twelve, that they should be with him, and that he might send them forth to preach" (Mark 3:14). Travel together, take vacations together, play sports together, do things together. What will take place is described in Proverbs 27:17: "Iron sharpeneth iron; so a man sharpeneth the countenance of his friend."

Ensure an Atmosphere of Acceptance

I remember when I was growing up that one of the things I appreciated about my father was the fact that I could always talk with him about any subject that was on my mind without fear of being misunderstood or reprimanded. The older I become the more precious this heritage becomes to me. It is something that I am working on with my own children.

Often there are things on our hearts that we would like to talk to someone about, but we are apprehensive simply because we are afraid of being misunderstood. When following up a Christian, it is essential that he feels free to share his doubts, fears, and personal problems no matter how intimate they may be, without feeling he will be condemned or rejected because of them.

Peter says, "Charity [love] shall cover the multitude of sins" (1 Peter 4:8). Probably no better counsel is to be found in how to overcome the feelings of inadequacy that all of us have, particularly in our interpersonal relationships. In meeting the needs of my wife, in raising my children, in helping others to mature in Christ, this feeling of inadequacy is sometimes overwhelming. But somehow it all turns out well by adding this ingredient called "love."

The apprehension you will feel in assuming responsibility for helping the new Christian is quite natural. The application of these simple principles will help, but will not eliminate all apprehension. Stick close by the person and love him as you would love a member of your own family. God will do the rest.

Chapter 8

HOW TO TRAIN A DISCIPLE—IMPARTING THE BASICS

As the disciple of Jesus Christ begins his disciple-making ministry, he finds before him a fivefold objective elaborated by the apostle Paul in 1 Thessalonians 1:5-10. Let's look at this passage to discover these key elements.

1. Solid decisions for Christ: "For our gospel came not unto you in word only, but also in power, and in the Holy Ghost, and in much assurance; as ye know what manner of men we were among you for your sake" (v. 5). When Paul preached the Gospel to the Thessalonians, the Word was proclaimed with power. It was accompanied by the Holy Spirit, and the result was that the people who came to Christ were filled with much assurance—they made solid decisions for Christ.

2. Disciples: "And ye became *followers of us, and of the Lord,* having received the word in much affliction with joy of the Holy Ghost" (v. 6). This is a rather useful definition of disciple: one who is a follower of us and of the Lord. People learn how to follow the Lord by following the Lord's people. Paul was able to disciple the Thessalonians because they were willing to follow him. Because Paul's life was consistent with the Scriptures and the leading of God, the Thessalonians became followers of the Lord as well.

3. Pacesetters: "So that *ye were ensamples* to all that believe in Macedonia and Achaia" (v. 7). The Thessalonians became a showcase for what it meant to be a Christian. Their lives were examples to the rest of the people in Greece.

4. Reproduction: "*For from you sounded out the word* of the Lord not only in Macedonia and Achaia, but also in every place your faith to God-ward [toward God] is spread abroad; *so that we need not to speak any thing*" (v. 8). Wherever Paul went, the response was, "We know exactly what you are talking about, for we met some of those Christians from Thessalonica." Paul's ministry to the Thessalonians was such that their immediate response was to share the Gospel with others.

5. Commitment: "*Ye turned to God from idols to serve the living and true God; and to wait for his Son* from heaven" (vv. 9-10). Notice what was involved:

- A turning *from* idolatry
- A turning *to* the true God
- Service, not passive profession of faith
- Expectation of Christ's glorious return

Thus far we have seen what is involved in bringing men to Christ and then following them up as new Christians. Now, what is involved in bringing people from the initial stages of follow-up to discipleship? We can call this the training process.

The Training Process

The dictionary defines train as "to direct the growth of; to form by instruction; discipline and drill; to form by bending; pruning, such as directing the growth of a plant."

In training we want to help people maximize their potential for Jesus Christ. In the training process, it must be remembered that the trainer cannot take upon himself the work of the Holy Spirit. He cannot reach down inside a person and change his sense of values— though often he wishes he could when he meets people who appear to be giving their lives to the wrong things, and whose sense of values seems to be warped.

All the trainer can do is help a disciple become what he wants to be. If a person does not see things from God's point of view, if he does not surrender his life to Jesus as Lord, if he is unwilling to pay the price of being Christ's servant, there is very little that can be done to disciple him. This is why the major part of this book is devoted to bringing the basic issues of life into focus. If a person is committed to Jesus Christ and highly motivated to do His will, the training process becomes simple, even enjoyable.

In the final analysis, the trainer can contribute to a person's development in only two areas: (1) the giving of time; (2) the opportunity to learn. All other factors conducive to change and growth—a feeling of personal responsibility, willingness to work sacrificially, attitudes of teachability and flexibility, native intelligence are either inherited or controlled by the person himself.

The trainer, therefore, must yield the total responsibility for change to the person he is training. He can, however, provide the person with a variety of training techniques which the person can use for his own self-development. The trainer then simply assumes the role of a guide and stimulus for the person, enabling him to attain his own goals and objectives.

There are many tools, techniques, and methods available in training people to become disciples. These should be clearly distinguished from principles, which have universal application. For example, Jesus said, "If ye continue in my word, *then* are ye my disciples indeed" (John 8:31). One of the principles of discipleship is to "continue in the Word." The various courses in Bible study and Scripture memory that are available are merely methods to help people continue in the Word. The fledgling disciple may be looking to you as the trainer for help in acquiring the best methods, but methodology should never be the primary goal and objective in the disciplemaking process.

In working with a young Christian, you might want to begin by asking him, "What is a disciple?" After he comes up with various possible definitions, you might further suggest, "Why don't we do a study in John's Gospel during this next week to see what it says?"

A week later you get together with him and go over what John's Gospel says a disciple is. Then you ask your Timothy, "Would you like to be a disciple?" Assuming his answer is yes, take the idea mentioned in John 8:31 about continuing in the Word and ask him to spend the next week thinking through how he can continue in the Word. Later, you will suggest various ways in which a person can get into the Word of God, but at this point don't tell your disciple what they are—let him discover them for himself.

At your next meeting, ask him to share with you the various ways one can get into the Word of God. After going over the things that he has discovered on his own, for his next assignment ask him to spend a week praying through what the Lord would have him do in each of these areas that he has listed. For example, he might have suggested Bible study, hearing the Word, reading the Word, and Scripture memory. His objective now is to find out what the Lord would have him to do in each of these areas.

The chances are that when you get together again, you will discover that the goals he has set for himself in these areas are far higher than any goals you would set for him. One of your jobs, therefore, will be to help him modify and keep realistic his own personal objectives. Whatever these objectives may be, they are his idea, the product of his prayerfully determining God's will for his life.

Help your disciple discover the principles of discipleship for himself through his study of the Word, and make sure that the applications he makes from these principles are his own.

As suggested in the chapter on follow-up, this type of individual instruction and coaching can only be done effectively on a one-to-one basis. Fellowship and group teaching will play a strategic role in augmenting the one-to-one ministry, but nothing can take the place of personal attention.

What Are the Basics?

A few years ago I was meeting with a person on a one-to-one basis, helping him to disciple his Timothy. As we talked about what this new Christian needed, the question arose, "What are the absolute essentials that must be present in an individual's life in order to consider him a disciple?" After batting this back and forth for awhile, we decided that we would do some personal study on it and discuss our findings. When we next met, we listed all the qualities we wanted to see in the person's life. By the time we were through, we had so many things on paper, it looked like a grocery list! We then decided that we had to make a distinction between the things we would like to see built into his life and those qualities that we felt were absolutely essential to a disciple.

We went back to work on the assignment once more, and came up with the same basics that a little illustration used by The Navigators (called the "Wheel") emphasizes.

WHEEL ILLUSTRATION—Reprinted with permission of The Navigators.

The Wheel is an illustration of the Christ-centered, Spirit-filled Christian walking in obedience.

The Hub of the Wheel

The hub of the Wheel is Jesus Christ. He is the center of everything. The apostle Paul explained this relationship when he wrote, "I am crucified with Christ: nevertheless I live; yet not I, but Christ liveth in me; and the life which I now live in the flesh I live by the faith of the Son of God, who loved me, and gave himself for me" (Gal. 2:20). The hub of a wheel does at least two things—it provides the power that moves the wheel, and it also gives direction for the wheel. This is the vital role that Jesus Christ plays in the life of the believer.

I remember once as a child watching a buddy of mine roll a spare car tire down a hill near our homes. As the tire went out of control, it rolled through peoples' yards, knocked down some flowers, hit a porch, bounced up, knocked over some Coke bottles, and finally landed in a neighbor's hedge. The problem with the tire was there was no direction given to it. Christ serving as the hub in the life of the Christian provides him with direction. Without Christ's direction, we are constantly in trouble, bumping into people, getting ourselves into difficulties, and causing damage.

The Spokes of the Wheel

1. The Word

The foundation spoke for the wheel is God's Word. Scripture says, "Let the word of Christ dwell in you richly in all wisdom;

teaching and admonishing one another in psalms and hymns and spiritual songs, singing with grace in your hearts to the Lord" (Col. 3:16).

Dawson Trotman, the founder of The Navigators, developed a simple illustration to show how the Word can be implemented in the Christian life. (Called the "Hand," this illustration appears below.) There are five main ways: hearing, reading, studying, memorizing, and meditating. All five must be functioning if one is to have a firm grasp on the Word.

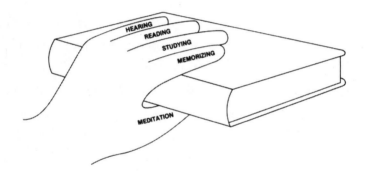

HAND ILLUSTRATION—Reprinted with permission of The Navigators.

• *Hear*—Help your disciple develop a regular hearing program. Suggest that he take notes in church as the pastor preaches. After the worship service, he can compare notes with others, talk about what was said, and seek ways to apply it. His pastor will probably be so startled to see him taking notes in church that he will have a coronary right there in the pulpit, but I am sure that he will recover from it and be encouraged to know that someone is giving such rapt attention to the Scriptures.

• *Read*—Encourage your disciple to adopt a plan for reading through the Scriptures once a year. By reading approximately three chapters a day, he can get through the Bible in the course of a year. There are many reading programs on the market, and you or his pastor can help him in locating one that will meet his needs. Reading through the Bible once a year will give him a panoramic view of the Scriptures. It will acquaint him with how God has worked through the ages.

• "*Study* to shew thyself approved unto God, a workman that needeth not to be ashamed, rightly dividing the word of truth" (2 Tim. 2:15). Bible study is the "meat and potatoes" of delving into the Word of God. There are five principles that all Bible studies should have irrespective of what method is employed. They are:

• *Original investigation*—The disciple and the Holy Spirit get together in the Word of God, and He assumes the role of instructor. The disciple may want to refer to Bible-study aids, but this is to be done only after he has completed his own original investigation

• *Consistency and system*—Bible study should not be a hit-and-miss program where the disciple studies a portion one week and then misses three months before studying another portion for a week. By system, I mean the disciple has a plan of attack rather than approaching the Scriptures in a haphazard fashion

• *Written reproduction*—The disciple writes his thoughts from the Bible study. Somebody once said, "Pale ink is better than the most retentive mind." All of us have had the unfortunate experience of losing a thought that we got from the Word simply because we failed to write it down

• *Pass-on-able*—Remember your objective is to have a continuing ministry of disciple-making "to the third and fourth generations." A friend of mine was sharing his Bible-study methodology—which included the use of several critical commentaries, Greek and Hebrew texts all incorporated into a rather elaborate approach. It was an impressive method he was using, but it was probably a trifle deficient in its "pass-on-ableness"

• *Application*—The Bible was not given primarily to increase our knowledge, but to change our lives. As Dr. Howard Hendricks, a professor at Dallas Theological Seminary, says, "Interpretation without application is abortion." In Bible study, we not only try to find out what Scripture says, but also what it says to *us*

You might find that answering the following questions on a passage provides a useful method of Bible study:

1. What does it say? Analyze the passage (either a paragraph or a chapter) verse by verse, jotting down any cross-references that come to mind. For example, if you were studying 2 Timothy 3:16 on the inspiration of Scripture, a possible cross-reference would be 2 Peter 1:21. Then list any observations or thoughts you might have on the passage

2. What does it say that I do not understand? Write down all the problems that you have with the passage. When I first began Bible study, I thought that the fewer problems I had, the better I understood the passage. The more I study the Scriptures, the more I realize that the converse is true. The deeper I probe into the passage, the more problems I have—that is, the more things in the chapter I realize I do not understand. Some of the questions you have will be answered in the course of your Bible study, some will be answered as you talk with others about them, and some may never fully be answered

3. What does it say in summary or outline? Either outline the chapter, giving its major divisions, or write a summary of the chapter. If you choose to write a summary, be careful that it does not become more wordy than the passage itself. Some have found it very helpful to apply both techniques—that is, to list the major divisions and then write a summary under each

4. What does it say to me? Write your personal application using this form: (a) state the problem; (b) give a specific example of the problem; (c) indicate the solution the Spirit of God would have you apply; (d) outline the specific steps you plan to take in applying the solution. Be careful to use only the personal pronouns: *I, me, my, mine.* Stay away from pronouns such as *we* and *us*

Remember, it is not *our* problem; it is *my* problem.

• *Memorize*—Probably no method of Scripture intake pays higher dividends for the time invested than Scripture memory. I have been memorizing the Scriptures on a consistent basis for a number of years now, and I regard it as being an extremely rewarding discipline, though at times demanding and exacting. Memorizing the verse itself is only a small portion of the task. Reviewing it a sufficient number of times so that you do not lose it constitutes most of the work.

There are many excellent Scripture-memory programs on the market, and I am sure your pastor can help you locate one that can satisfactorily meet your needs. One that I have found most useful is *The Topical Memory System,* published by The Navigators, because the program is designed to teach you how to memorize the Scriptures on your own.

• *Meditate*—This is the thumb in the Hand illustration and finds its application with the other four fingers. You hear the Word and meditate on it, read the Word and meditate on it, study and meditate, memorize and meditate. Meditation drives the passage home, fixes it in the mind, and helps you formulate application.

If I am only hearing the Word of God and meditating on it, it's like trying to hold the Bible with one finger and a thumb; I have a poor grasp of it. If, however, I am hearing and reading the Word of God while meditating on it, I have a slightly better grasp, though not yet sufficient. As I implement each of the various means of Scripture intake, I have an increasingly stronger grip on the sword of the Spirit. It is not until I have all five fingers in operation that I have a truly good grip on the Word of God.

2. Prayer

This spoke lies opposite to the Word and plays a balancing role with the Word in the Christian life. The person who is strong in the Word but weak in prayer is like a skeleton; there is no flesh on it. The person who is strong in prayer but weak in the Word is like a fleshy person with no skeleton—just like a jellyfish. The Word and prayer together form the proper balance in the Christian's life.

Prayer does not require a great deal of methodology; it is simply conversing with God. But because of its strategic role in the Christian life, the devil does his utmost to discourage its practice. If you are weak in prayer, get yourself a prayer partner, somebody who will pray with you at regular, appointed times. I remember when in college I realized my weakness in this area, and so I talked a buddy of mine into praying every week with me. We would meet in an empty dorm room at 11:00 in the morning and pray until 4:00 in the afternoon. I cannot remember all the things we prayed for, but I do know that it was an extremely profitable exercise in helping to build the habit of prayer into my life.

One of the most motivating little booklets that I have read on the subject of prayer is E.M. Bounds' *Power through Prayer.* I would highly recommend it for your reading and application.

3. Witnessing

Another hallmark of a disciple is that witnessing is an integral part of his life. The last words of the Lord Jesus to His disciples were, "But you shall receive power when the Holy Spirit has come upon you; and you shall be My witnesses both in Jerusalem, and in all Judea and Samaria, and even to the remotest part of the earth" (Acts 1:8 NASB). Witnessing is one of those tasks we try to avoid, but after we get into a witnessing situation, the thrill and excitement is such that we wonder why we hesitated in the first place.

Probably one of the greatest fears people have in witnessing is the fear of being rejected. "He doesn't want to listen to me," we rationalize. "He is probably busy and preoccupied with something else. Anyway, he might become offended and rebuke me for talking with him about spiritual matters." Yet, when, if ever, have you spoken to somebody about the Lord Jesus and found him to be offended? Usually people are very warm and eager to talk about spiritual matters.

Several years ago I was helping a young man who was extremely reluctant to witness. He was involved in beginning a student ministry, so I asked him, "Joe, how many students on campus do you know personally? By that I mean, when they see you, they know you by name."

After having been there for a couple of months, he knew only two or three men. I said, "Joe, in the next four weeks, I want you to get to know as many students on campus as you can. Let's set our goal at fifty students. You don't have to witness to them. You don't even have to tell them you are a Christian. All you have to do is get to know them. Stop by their rooms and chat with them. Play table tennis with them. Go to athletic events with them. Go to meals together. Do anything you want, but get to know fifty men so that one month from today, when I return, you can introduce me to each one of them by name."

One month later I returned to visit Joe on the campus and found that he had led six men to Christ. We didn't talk about whether he had gotten to know fifty people. We didn't have to. He had discovered for himself that as he became friends with "the publicans and sinners," the Lord naturally provided opportunities for him to share his faith. Witnessing, then, begins by establishing friendships with nonChristians. As these friendships mature, the Holy Spirit will provide opportunities to witness.

As you train your disciple, take him into your environment for his witnessing experiences. Introduce him to your nonChristian friends, and let him watch you in action as you share your faith. Then as he gains confidence, he will feel comfortable doing the same thing with his own nonChristian friends.

I remember another occasion when working with students on campus that I had a young man on my team who was very apprehensive about talking to others about Christ. I could get Bill to do Bible study and Scripture memory, but I just could not get him to witness.

After several months of persuasion, Bill reluctantly agreed to join me in sharing the Gospel with somebody as long as he did not have to do any talking. We went out and talked to a friend of mine about the Lord. We repeated this a number of times with different people until eventually Bill gained enough confidence to join in the conversation. As the weeks passed, he became more and more at ease, and soon the time came for him to share the Gospel with one of his buddies. I went along simply as an observer; this time he was going to do all the talking.

We got to Ron's room and chatted for a few minutes, and then Bill changed the topic of conversation and began sharing the Gospel. As I listened, I realized to my horror that Bill was doing everything wrong. His approach was backward. He was using all the wrong verses. He broke every "rule" in the book! It was so bad that I had to bite my tongue to keep myself from butting into the conversation and "rescuing" him.

After what seemed to me to be several long and very embarrassing minutes, Bill said, "Well, Ron, do you want to receive Christ or not?"

"Boy, I sure do," came the unexpected reply.

As I knelt there with them beside Ron's bed, I felt as if I was in a dream. I simply could not believe my ears. Ron had just prayed and received Christ! And as Bill followed him up in the subsequent months, Ron proved to be a disciple in his own right.

What a lesson the Holy Spirit taught me. Evangelism is God's work—not man's. And the Holy Spirit will take the most feeble efforts of people and use them to bring Christ into the seeking heart.

4. Fellowship

In the next chapter, we will talk about the development of people's gifts and their use in the body. Fellowship around the Word in prayer, with Christ as the center, is crucial to the Christian life. Draw your disciple into the fellowship of like-minded believers who can help edify him. A great deal need not be said here about fellowship, for it plays a large role in the average Christian's life so much so that if we are not careful it will become disproportionately large in relation to the rest of the "spokes."

The spokes of a wheel must all be in balance for the wheel to rotate smoothly without vibrating. Any one spoke should not be heavier or play a more prominent role in the life of the disciple than another. Furthermore, the longer the spokes, the greater the circumference of the wheel and the more ground covered with each revolution. The disciple's goal is to build up each of the spokes.

Another thing that can be said of the spokes is that they provide the only contact that the hub has with the rim. The Christian is in contact with Jesus Christ through the spokes. Two of them, the Word and prayer, deal with intake; and two of them, witnessing and fellowship, deal with output. Someone has observed, "If your output exceeds your intake, then your upkeep becomes your downfall." This very clearly expresses the importance of balance in the Christian life.

The Rim of the Wheel

Jesus said, "He who has My commandments, and keeps them, he it is who loves Me; and he who loves Me shall be loved of My Father, and I will love him, and will manifest Myself to him" (John 14:21).

Obedience is the outgrowth of a disciple's life. It is this life of obedience that is most visible to the world.

A young man from India was studying at one of our universities, and another student witnessed to him about the claims of Christ. The Indian had observed how Christians were living, and his response was, "What you Christians are speaks so loudly that I cannot hear what you are saying." These Christians did not walk their talk.

Just as the spokes provide the only contact that the rim has with the hub, so the rim is the only contact that Jesus Christ has with the world. The only Christ that the nonbelieving world can see is the Christ inside each Christian. When people look at you, do they see Christ reflected in your life?

In addition to using the Wheel illustration to help you train your disciple, you might want to develop some areas of character, such as purity of life, faith, love, and integrity. However, we must constantly remind ourselves that the implementation of our training objectives must be done in synchronization with the individual's needs.

On the basis of these needs, develop a plan. Always ask yourself three questions: (1) What does he need? (2) How can he get it? (3) How will I know when he has it? These three questions can be asked in a variety of ways. For instance: (1) Where am I going? (2) How am I going to get there? (3) How will I know when I have arrived? Whatever way you wish to phrase them, always ask the same three questions.

Let's apply this plan to a specific issue: *faith*. The answer to question one is faith. Question two, however, is far more difficult, particularly in a subjective area like faith. Here you will need some creative thinking. There might be some books you would like to have him read that would build his faith. You certainly will want to include prayer in your plan, both on your part and on his. Have him memorize some verses on the subject of faith. Help him in a guided experience by choosing some area in his life where he can really trust God—maybe in the financial realm, or for another disciple with whom he can work. As you plan, ask God for a sanctified imagination!

Question three is probably the most difficult since it has to do with evaluating. Without it, however, you will never know if and when you have reached your objective. Whatever plan you incorporate, it should have built into it some measuring technique that will let you know the degree to which you have accomplished your goal.

The plan that you develop for each area you want to work on with your disciple should be a very flexible thing. The temptation to rigidly apply it should be steadfastly resisted. Whatever plan you develop, keep it to yourself to create as much spontaneity as possible. Do not form the person to the plan, but rather form the plan to the person.

Helping the Disciple Transmit to Others

The training process does not merely consist of sharing information. Rather, it involves helping people with the "how to" of discipleship so that they can implement a vision. With this in mind, at the earliest possible opportunity encourage your disciple to begin discipling another. This will do several things for him:

1. It will solidify his own convictions.

More often than not when the disciple begins relating to another the truths of Christianity, he is asked penetrating questions. His formation of answers tends to seal the truths to his own heart as well as help the other person.

2. It provides a laboratory for his own growth.

As he builds into the life of another disciple, he has the opportunity to see whether what he himself does is applicable to others.

3. It makes him teachable and eager to learn.

With his own disciple asking awkward questions, it will make him all the more desirous to learn more himself. A friend of mine was teaching artillery at Fort Sill, Oklahoma just after the Korean War. The young officers in his classroom were inattentive and frequently fell asleep in the middle of his lectures. Several years later, he found himself teaching the same subject at Fort Sill, this time in the middle of the Vietnam War. None of the men in his class were inattentive; none fell asleep; everyone was asking questions and giving him undivided attention. The reason for the marked contrast is quite simple. In the latter case there was a war going on, and the men knew that as soon as they finished their instruction, they would be shipped over to Vietnam to fight. For the first group, the war was already over.

Things to Remember in the Discipling Process

There is so much involved in the training process that it would take several volumes to treat the subject in a comprehensive way. It is my prayer, however, that this chapter will act as a catalyst in your own mind and cause you to do some experimenting. There are some common sense "do's and don'ts" that are applicable in any interpersonal relationship. Here are a few of the more obvious ones for you to apply in your disciple-making ministry:

1. Remember he belongs to God.

It is God's ministry, and God must do the building in your disciple's life. All you can ever hope to be is a tool in God's hands. "Unless the LORD builds the house, they labor in vain who build it; unless the LORD guards the city, the watchman keeps awake in vain" (Ps. 127:1 NASB).

2. He must know that you believe in him and that you have confidence in him.

Don't ever give him a job and then take it away from him.

3. Do not allow him to become dependent on you.

Train him with independence in mind. Your job is to help him learn from God. Don't tie him to your apron strings.

4. Allow him the freedom to fail.

In the business world, many executives learn more through their failures than through their successes; and yet, the greatest fear that most people have is the fear of failure. Let your disciple know that he can fail without fear of rejection from you.

5. Teach him how to evaluate potential disciples.

Jesus did not rush into choosing the Twelve. His choice of disciples took place only after He was firmly planted in His ministry.

Paul says, "Lay hands suddenly on no man, neither be partaker of other men's sins: keep thyself pure" (1 Tim. 5:22).

6. Seek to instill confidence.

A disciple must learn to believe in himself. "I am crucified with Christ: nevertheless I live; yet not I, but Christ lives in me: and the life which I now live in the flesh I live by the faith of the Son of God, who loved me, and gave himself for me" (Gal. 2:20). In this verse we see two "I's"—the crucified "I" and the resurrected "I." In training we often work hard at crucifying the "old I" but spend little time in helping a disciple resurrect the "new I" in Christ. We must have "no confidence in the flesh," but at the same time believe that, "I can do all things through Christ."

Summary

Making disciples takes time. It cannot be done through a series of lectures and a training seminar in the church, nor can it be done by reading a book. It cannot be rushed. One of the dominant characteristics of our modern culture is our ability and desire to mass-produce. We mass-produce everything—cars, appliances, furniture, pots and pans, and household gadgets. We have even become proficient in mass-producing houses! It is so easy to take this "mass-produced mentality" and apply it to disciple-making. It cannot be done. Disciples are made, but not mass-produced. Each one is molded and fashioned individually by the Spirit of God.

How long it takes is a matter of conjecture and varies from person to person, depending to a large degree on where they are when they begin the training process. But one thing is certain; it does take time. The Lord Jesus began with 12 monotheistic, God-fearing men, who came from reasonably good homes. He devoted Himself fulltime to their training and development. He was a Master at the art of training, and yet it took Him three full years. We can hardly hope to do it in less.

Chapter 9

HOW TO TRAIN A DISCIPLE—CONVICTION AND PERSPECTIVE

Baseball, like most other sports, has its "Hall of Fame." In Oklahoma City, one can walk through the "Cowboy Hall of Fame." On the right is Will Rogers, and down a ways are Buffalo Bill and many others, men who carved out the West, heroes of what has become the American way of life. Hebrews 11 is God's "Hall of Fame"—the heroes of the faith. As you walk through its corridors, you see heroes and heroines of a bygone age—men and women from all walks of life but with one thing in common; they believed God!

Faith, simply defined, is "believing the promises of God and acting on them." It is obeying the promises of God. Faith is never passive—always active. Note the action verbs in the chapter. Abel *offered* (v. 4), Noah *prepared* (v. 7), Abraham *obeyed* (v. 8).

But faith without a commitment on God's part is not faith at all; it is presumption. God had made some pretty fantastic promises to the people mentioned in Hebrews 11, and they acted on them. Without these promises from God, their actions would have been without reason.

Let us imagine that you and I are flying in a small aircraft at 10,000 feet. I ask you, "Could God catch me if I jumped?"

With a note of hesitation you answer, "I … I'm not sure."

Believing that you are expressing a lack of faith, I say, "I believe He can," and then I jump. On my way down, I realize to my horror that though my statement is true, "God can catch me," He never promised that He would. I die not because of a lack of faith but because of the lack of a promise from God. I was presumptuous. Faith must have a basis for its existence.

Before a person is willing to commit himself to act on what God has promised, two things must be true. He must have *conviction* and *perspective*. These attributes are readily seen in the life of Moses as described in Hebrews 11.

Verse 23:

> By faith Moses, when he was born, was hid three
> months of [by] his parents, because they saw *he was*
> *a* proper [beautiful] child; and they were not afraid
> of the king's commandment.

Notice that faith as it relates to the life of Moses began with Mom and Dad. Moses was a baby. He couldn't act on the promises of God. It was his parents' faith that saved the day.

Verse 24:

> By faith Moses, when he was come to years, refused
> to be called the son of Pharaoh's daughter.

Previously, it was the faith of Moses' parents; now it is the faith of Moses. How did this happen? When did it become his faith? "When he was come to years."

I imagine when Moses was growing up, he mimicked the essentials of godly faith with great enthusiasm because of what he heard from his mother. (You will remember after the daughter of Pharaoh found Moses, she turned him over to his own mother to be nursed.) To hear a small child say, "Jesus lives in my heart" is cute, even though this may be simply an expression of the parents' faith. But there comes a time in each of our lives when it is no longer valid to base what we believe on the convictions held by others. When we "come to years," our lives must be based on our own convictions. Moses believed in the same God in verse 24 that his parents did in verse 23, but they were his own convictions, the result of his own personal experience with God.

Look at verses 24-27. He refused to be called the son of Pharaoh's daughter. He chose to suffer affliction with the people of God rather than to enjoy the pleasures of sin for a season. He forsook Egypt. These were actions based on Moses' own convictions.

When we enter into training, what we do in the initial stages is largely determined by the person who is helping us. The things that a small child says and believes are basically dependent on what she hears from her parents. It is fun listening to her pray. Because she does not understand the meanings of the words, she mixes them up, parroting phrases she has heard other people use.

So it is for the new Christian. Often he prays before meals or goes to church not because of his own personal convictions, but because others have suggested this is what he ought to do. This is not necessarily bad. Having come to Christ through the influence of another, it is natural that he continues by doing what others suggest.

There comes a time, however, when such reasons for doing things are no longer valid. He must eventually arrive at his own convictions. Knowing what to do and how to do it is important, and has been given a lot of emphasis in this book. But knowing what to do and how to do it must be superseded by a personal conviction that this is what God wants me to do.

Joe Marine goes through boot camp at Parris Island, South Carolina, or Camp Lejeune, North Carolina. After eight weeks of training, the commanding officer has a general inspection. If we were to follow the commanding officer, how would we find Joe's bed? Perfectly made, with the blanket so neat and tight you could bounce a quarter off of it. The locker? Immaculate, with everything exactly in its place. And the bathroom? So clean you would think it had never been used.

Four years go by and Joe Marine is now a sophomore at the University of California. We visit him in his room. How do we find his bed? As if it had never been made. His locker? A shambles. How about the bathroom? So bad that it reminds you of a restroom in a rundown gas station in the most backward part of the country.

Why the difference? It is not that Joe does not know what to do, or how to do it. Joe's problem is that he has no conviction that he should continue doing it after leaving the Marine Corps.

Many Christians have neither the convictions nor the methods needed to disciple others. But if a choice had to be made between conviction and method, conviction is the more important by far. (I say if because I do not believe such a choice is necessary. I call for the choice here only to emphasize the importance of conviction.)

Discover the person who has the conviction without knowing how to disciple others, and you will eventually see that person find the method. Give a person all the methodology in the world and, if he lacks conviction, eventually he will stop discipling others, no matter how careful you have been in imparting the methods. The person who has methods without conviction is like a bouquet of cut flowers—he is impressive to look at, but he will not last!

Back to the story of Moses in Hebrews 11:

Verse 26:

> Considering the reproach of Christ greater riches than the treasures of Egypt; for he [Moses] was looking to the reward. (NASB)

J.B. Phillips renders the last part of this verse, "For he looked steadily at the ultimate, not the immediate, reward." That is perspective—the ability to see the end from the beginning. We can call it bifocal vision—the ability to see what is directly in front of us in light of the long-range.

The person who has things in perspective makes his decisions on the immediate in light of the ultimate. Of the two arch stones in training, *conviction* is one, *perspective,* the other.

Perspective is seeing it like it is. It has to do with a person's philosophy of life, what is important to him, his sense of values, the things that motivate him. Jesus said,

> Consider the ravens: for they neither sow nor reap; which neither have storehouse nor barn; and God feedeth them. How much more are ye better than the fowls? And which of you with taking thought can add to his stature one cubit? If ye then be not able to do that thing which is least, why take ye thought for the rest? Consider the lilies how they grow: they toil not, they spin not; and yet I say to you, that Solomon in all his glory was not arrayed like one of these. If then God so clothe the grass, which is to day in the field, and to morrow is cast into the oven; how much more *will he clothe* you, O ye of little faith? And seek not you what ye shall eat, or what ye shall drink, neither be ye of doubtful mind. For all these things do the nations of the world seek after: and your Father knows that ye have need of these things. But rather seek ye the kingdom of God; and all these things shall be added unto you. Fear not, little flock; for it is your Father's good pleasure to give you the kingdom. Sell that ye have, and give alms; provide yourselves bags which

wax not old, a treasure in the heavens that faileth
not, where no thief approacheth, neither moth cor-
rupteth. For where your treasure is, there will your
heart be also. (Luke 12:24-34)

This is a perfect example of perspective: seeing it like it is, the
end from the beginning. Here Jesus is urging us to make present
decisions in light of ultimate results.

The only time a person willfully sins is when his perspective goes
out of focus. He deceives himself into believing he can sin and get
away with it. A man walks into a bank and robs it of $100,000. If he
could have visualized himself spending the next 25 years in an 8' x
12' cage, do you think he would have done it? No! He robs the bank
because he cannot see the consequences of his act. He lacks perspective. This is the case each time we sin.

Conviction and perspective characterized the life of Moses. They
are the two most important aspects of the training process. They are
essential ingredients in "The Art of Discipling." If the aspirant lacks
either conviction or perspective, he is not trained.

How do you develop conviction and perspective? How do you
build them into your own life, and how do you build them into the
life of another? The psalmist says, "Except the LORD build the house,
they labour in vain that build it: except the LORD keep the city, the
watchman waketh *but* in vain" (Ps. 127:1). Training begins and ends
with God. If He is not at work in us "to will and do of His good
pleasure," we labor in vain. God imparts conviction and perspective.

Having said this, however, there are certain guidelines that can
help us in exercising our responsibility. I will mention four of them

for your consideration and application. These four are by no means exhaustive. You may want to amplify them and add more of your own.

Major in Principles Rather Than Methods.

In this, as well as in the other three guidelines, the phrase "rather than" is not meant to connote "either … or." It is not principle *or* method, one to the exclusion of the other; it is both principle *and* method. But in building conviction and perspective, we want to *major* in principle rather than method. It is a matter of emphasis.

In Jesus' Parable of the Sower (Luke 8), He tells why the seed is sown, what takes place, and when. But He does not mention *how* to sow the seed. The "how" is left up to us. Jesus is dealing with principles, not methods.

The Great Commission is another example. The command is to go into all the world and preach the Gospel to every creature. Jesus said to begin at Jerusalem, Samaria, Judea, and then move out into the rest of the world. His life and ministry are an example of how to do it. Mark 3:14 says, "And he ordained twelve, that they should be with him, and that he might send them forth to preach." From Jesus' example, we can see the best way to do the job is to select a few people and invest our time and our very lives in them.

But the actual method, the nitty-gritty of working it out, was left up to the disciples. The Book of Acts is the methodology of how these men sought to obey Christ's Great Commission. Most of what they did was the application of principles taught them by Jesus. We read in Acts 6 that the widows had been neglected. The

method the disciples employed to meet that need was the appoint-
ing of deacons. The office of deacon was not something Jesus in His
earthly ministry urged them to initiate. It was a method used by
them to meet a need.

As Christians, we have our methodology. We may have a worship
service and Sunday school in the morning and have another service
in the evening. Each denomination has its own way of doing things:
its order of worship, method of baptism, doctrinal instruction, and
Sunday school curriculum. And all of this may be right and good.
There is *nothing* wrong with having methods.

If, however, we follow our methodology because of tradition
("we have always done it this way") rather than because of carefully
thought-out principles, we close our minds to new and better ways.
Change becomes a threat. But if biblical principles form the basis
for what we do, then we will be eager for new and better ways of
doing it.

Let me draw an illustration from the kitchen. My wife has a
certain way of washing dishes. First into the suds go the glasses, then
the silverware, followed by the plates, then the bowls, and finally
the pots and pans. This is her method of washing dishes. But I had
no conviction that I should wash dishes that way. One day I began
with the pans—and she corrected me. While discussing why I should
begin with the glasses, she pointed out that the objective in washing
is to sterilize the things being washed. If getting the food off were all
we wanted, we could let the dog lick them. They were washed to sterilize them—this was the principle. Therefore, it follows that it is best
to wash first those things which have contact with the mouth and last
those utensils which will have a chance to sterilize themselves.

As a result of this, I always wash the glasses first, then the silverware, and so on. I no longer do it this way just because my wife is watching. Having understood the principle behind the method, I developed my own conviction. Convictions are built, not by practicing the method, but by understanding the principle.

The would-be disciple sees things clearly (perspective) and develops convictions by probing into the whys of what is done. And yet, frequently, why is an irritating question, often hard to answer. In training, resist the temptation to gloss over the why. Probe deeply. Ask such questions as: "Is this the best way to have a quiet time?" "Why do we believe Bible study is necessary?" "What are the implications of possible alternatives?" Such probing helps build perspective and conviction.

Major in Meeting the Needs of Others Rather Than in Developing and Imparting Techniques.

Jesus and His disciples walk down the steps of the temple. Before them is a blind man. His need is obvious. If I had been there with Jesus, I probably would have whipped out a tract and begun witnessing, only to realize suddenly that the man could not follow what I was doing. He could not see!

Jesus' approach was different. Squatting down beside him, He spat on the ground, made some mud, and rubbed it on the blind man's eyes. "Go, wash in the pool of Siloam," was the command, and "he went … washed, and came seeing" (John 9:7).

You will notice that the man eventually did find salvation, but Jesus began by meeting his need.

Many a Christian views training as sitting in a classroom situation, learning how to master some techniques. He learns how to teach a Sunday school curriculum, how to make a financial presentation to another member of the congregation, or even how to pass out a piece of literature and follow it up with a Gospel presentation. In the last illustration, more often than not the person to whom you "witness" does not respond and so you become discouraged and head back for another training session, or possibly you quit altogether. The person does not respond because you are not addressing yourself to the point of his felt need. He has no conviction he should pursue the conversation further and, because you do not get the anticipated response, you do not see the use of continuing such a futile exercise.

While I was ministering to students in Michigan, the Lord gave a great deal of fruit. Christian students living in the dorms with non-Christian friends related well with them. They went to class, meals, football games, and elsewhere together. Relationships were formed that became natural bridges for communicating the Gospel. Every so often we would have a pizza party or an "Andrew dinner" at our house and would have the privilege of seeing a number of people come to Christ.

Hearing of these and similar successes on other campuses, a church in Ohio asked a group of us to come down and become involved with them in an evangelistic thrust. They decided to invite their friends to a "neutral" spot and to share a testimony or two before giving a short Gospel presentation. When the time came, many from the congregation showed up, but not one nonChristian. All had invited someone, but no one had responded.

As we sat together analyzing why this had happened, it soon became apparent that, though many of the people had nonChristian acquaintances, not one had a nonChristian friend. So, when approached, the "acquaintances" were hesitant in accepting.

How then do you become friends with an unbeliever and discern his needs? Let me offer a few suggestions:

• *Be a good listener.* We live in an age when everyone wants to talk and no one wants to listen. When others find out that you are willing to listen, it is amazing how much talking they will do. Often in an accepting atmosphere they will expose their needs and reveal their concerns.

Have you ever talked to someone and found that he had turned on his "uh huh"? As you talk, he says, "Uh huh, uh huh, uh huh." As you draw others out, do not turn on your "uh huh." Be a good listener.

• *Share your own needs, weaknesses, and experiences.* Do not make your friend feel as though he stands alone. The Bible says, "There hath no temptation taken you but such as is common to man" (1 Cor. 10:13). Admit this to be true in your own life. By sharing your shortcomings, an accepting atmosphere will be created in which others will feel free to share theirs.

In Amarillo, Texas, a group of men get together each week for prayer and fellowship in somebody's home. They read a passage of Scripture and discuss it in light of their needs. Believers and unbelievers come together as friends sharing common concerns. The Christians make sure to avoid the impression of "we" and "they." Instead they talk about "our" problems, "our" struggles, "our" sins. Then together they pray over them. As a result, men are consistently coming to know Christ as Savior.

• *Spend time together.* Invite your friends over for dinner. Join them at their parties. Go fishing together. As relationships are built, barriers come down. A true friendship means mutual acceptance of one another. If I accept him the way he is, a freedom will exist between us that will allow the sharing of mutual needs and concerns.

As these needs are exposed, it will become very natural to talk about how Christ shares your life. These are just three possibilities, and a flood of other ideas may have already come to your mind.

Meeting needs is how conviction and perspective come, both to the trainer and the trainee. As you and your nonChristian friends discuss the essentials of the Christian life, you will be amazed how issues will come into focus for you, and doctrines that were once theological jargon will become deep-seated convictions.

Major in Developing the Thought Processes Rather Than the Skills.

Jesus Christ is far more interested in what we are than what we do. "It is for you to be; it is for God to do," provides a simple but wise piece of advice. The Savior wants to reprogram our computer, to change our whole thought process.

What was His one complaint with the Pharisees? That they did not know how to evangelize? Jesus Himself said they would cross the sea to proselyte one individual. That they did not know the Word of God? They studied it regularly. They tithed their income, prayed, and fasted regularly. From all outward appearances, they were good men.

Proverbs 23:7 says, "As he thinketh in his heart, so *is* he." This is where Jesus found fault with them. It had to do with their philosophy of life, the way they thought. Their problem was seen in their attitude, their sense of values, their whole outlook on life.

A partial list of concepts that indicate an inner change includes: not feeling the need to shape your own destiny because you trust God's sovereign control over your life; being a servant; submitting to the authority of others; looking after the interests of others at the expense of your own. You may want to make your own list of concepts you feel are essential for the disciple of Jesus Christ.

Often such changes in the thinking process come slowly and subtly. Not until we have a point of comparison do they become evident. A friend of mine, training in the Christian life in California, said it was not until he went home months later and began interacting with old friends that he realized how great the changes in his life were.

Many people think of training as the imparting of ideas or skills which takes place in the classroom through a pupil-teacher relationship. What we are talking about here has to do with the imparting of character—the changing of a person's sense of values.

The world says, "Get all you can, can all you get, and poison the rest."

God says, "Give without any thought of getting.'

The world says, "Shop for a mate."

God says, "Trust me to provide you a spouse in My time.'

The world says, "Climb the ladder of success, even if it means stepping on others in the process."

God says, "Do not look after your own interests, but the interests of others."

These kinds of changes in a person's life are of great importance to God, more so than the acquiring of skills such as a particular Bible-study technique. Major in bringing the philosophy of life into conformity with the Bible, and the convictions and perspective will naturally follow.

Major in How to Trust God Rather Than Teaching Theories about God.

Earlier in this chapter, we talked briefly about the Parable of the Sower (Luke 8). Let us go back and take another look at it. It can equally well be called, "The Parable of the Four Soils," or "The Parable of the Four Responses to God's Word."

The first response to God's Word is *no faith*. Verse 12 says the devil "taketh away the word out of their hearts, lest they should believe and be saved."

The second response to the Word is *faith without conviction*. "They on the rock *are they*, which, when they hear, receive the word with joy; and these have no root, which for a while believe, and in time of temptation fall away" (v. 13). Such people give mental assent to the Word, but when times of testing and sacrifice come, they "abandon ship." They lack the *conviction* that Christianity is worthy of the cost.

The third response is seen in verse 14. "And that which fell among thorns are they, which, when they have heard, go forth, and are choked with cares and riches and pleasures of *this* life, and bring no fruit to perfection." This is faith without perspective. After receiving the Word, such people confuse their priorities.

What was once important in life goes out of focus, and they give their lives to insignificance. Mediocrity is the by-product of a lack of perspective.

Verse 15 gives us the final response to God's Word. "But that on the good ground are they, which in an honest and good heart, having heard the word, keep *it,* and bring forth fruit with patience." Such people take God at His Word and act accordingly. This fourth illustration is the only proper response to God's Word—*reproductive faith.*

So, the issue of the parable is: no faith, faith without conviction, faith without perspective, and reproductive faith. After this brief lecture on faith, Jesus moves out into real-life situations, giving the disciples an opportunity to see what it means to walk by faith. The rest of Luke 8 can be divided as follows:

VERSES 22-25—Crossing the stormy sea
VERSES 26-39—Maniac in the land of the Gadarenes
VERSES 40-56—Raising of Jairus' daughter
VERSES 43-48—Healing of woman with an issue of blood

In all of these life situations, Jesus is trying to communicate the importance of faith. The pattern in each of the stories is basically the same:

1. A need arises
2. Jesus intervenes and promises to meet that need
3. No sooner is the promise made than seeming disaster strikes

4. Jesus responds by urging the person to trust Him: "Only believe."/"Have faith"

The daughter of Jairus is sick. Jesus promises to meet the need. The daughter dies. Jesus says, "Fear not: believe only, and she shall be made whole" (v. 50). Jesus was not interested in people mastering the different theories on the attributes of God. He wanted people to learn to trust God.

Who do you imagine knew the most about God? Abraham in the Old Testament or a modern-day theologian? Let me suggest it would be the theologian of today. Abraham could not have told you about the two advents of Christ; nor could he have explained the differences between the pre-, post-, and amillennial positions; nor the dual nature of Christ; nor the Virgin Birth; nor a dozen other points of theology.

But Abraham knew God! He has a singular place in Scripture as a man who pleased God. In the New Testament alone, he is mentioned 74 times. "Abraham believed God, and it was accounted to him for righteousness" (Gal. 3:6). God was so pleased with this man that Hebrews 11:16 says, "God is not ashamed to be called [his] God."

It is one thing for you to be known by God. It is entirely different for God to be known by you. The Creator God of heaven and earth says, "I am the God of Abraham." Fantastic! The Creator is known by the creature. "If you want to know what I am like," says God, "take a look at Abraham." Can the living God be known by you? Can God say, "If you want to know what I am like, just look at the life of the person reading this book"?

We have said that in training disciples you should:

1. Major in principles rather than methods
2. Major in meeting the needs of people rather than on developing, and imparting techniques
3. Major in developing the thought processes rather than the skills
4. Major in how to trust God rather than teaching theories about God

By now, you may realize that these four suggestions are simply four facets of the same truth, like the facets of a diamond. The gem we are looking at is conviction and perspective.

Somebody once said ninety percent of the Christian life is survival. This may or may not be. But if survival is your objective in the Christian life, you will fail. You are like a boxer who enters the ring knowing only how to defend himself. He cannot possibly win. He needs a good attack as well.

For the Christian, an attack is another word for a plan or objective. An aggressive attack in your walk with God requires conviction and perspective, and these are hard to come by. Training is hard. But remember, training means growing, and growing means stretching. Growing never has been and never will be a pleasant experience. This is why babies cry. A child learning how to walk falls down and hurts himself often. You say to him, "Get up and try again."

Does he say, "No, I have tried it several times, and it does not work. I think I will just lie here for the rest of my life"? No, he has to get up and try it again. My son fell so many times we called him "Scar Face."

Growing is so painful a process that the first chance we get, we want to stop. But there are certain pressures that keep the young person growing. Physical growth itself is one. My daughter once said to me, "Dad, I have done all the growing I want. I like my age and size; I think I will stop here." The trouble was, she could not stop growing just because she wanted to. Biologically, she was forced to grow. The state laws also force us to grow. A child may want to quit school in the fifth grade. But the law says he cannot. And finally, there is the pressure of a society which expects a person to be able to care for himself—he is expected to learn a trade or profession.

By the time a person is in his mid-twenties, these pressures ease a bit. We have probably done all the physical growing we will do. Our education is behind us, and we have learned how to make a living. So great is the temptation to stop growing that, when we graduate from high school or college, they call it "commencement." Anything to encourage us to keep growing. But our desire to escape the pain of growth is, in most instances, too great an obstacle to overcome. We begin to coast for the rest of our lives on past experience. Having begun well, we drift into mediocrity.

Perspective and conviction (the ability to see the end from the beginning, and a deep-seated belief regarding what is on the heart of God) are the only things I know that will check this natural inclination.

John W. Gardner in his book, *Excellence,* says,

> We fall into the error of thinking that happiness necessarily involves ease, diversion, tranquility—a state in which all of one's wishes are satisfied. For most people, happiness is not to be found in this vegetative state but in striving toward meaningful

goals. For dedicated men and women, life is the endless pursuit of goals, some of them unattainable. Such people may often be tense, worried, fatigued. They may have little of the leisure one associates with the storybook conception of happiness. But the truth is that happiness in the sense of total gratification is not a state to which humans can aspire. It is for cows, possibly for the birds, but not for us.[1]

The arch stones of training to be Christ's disciples are conviction and perspective. They make the difference between the "finisher" and the "also ran." It was not easy for Moses, and it will not be for you. Moses spent the first forty years of his life in the palace of Pharaoh. The next forty years were spent on the backside of the desert squeezing sand between his toes as he took care of another man's sheep. The last forty years were spent wandering in the wilderness suffering with his own generation. After such a brilliant start, what a seemingly miserable end. Everything in him must have wanted to quit. But he did not give in. He hung in there and became a finisher. As a result, the whole world knows about Moses. Every Arab, Jew, and Christian knows about Moses. Every educated person in the world knows about the great lawgiver.

Moses' life of seeming frustration and failure was in reality a success. Why did he finish so well? It was because he had conviction and perspective.

Chapter 10

HOW TO TRAIN A DISCIPLE—GIFTS AND CALLING

Just before His death on Calvary, the Lord Jesus expressed to His Father what was on His heart. In that prayer, recorded in John 17, we find one of His major concerns was that Christians dwell together in unity.

The Holy Spirit's bestowal of gifts on the church was designed to ensure that our Lord Jesus' prayer for unity would be answered. He did this by making sure that all Christians have some of the gifts, and no Christian has all of the gifts. This assured the importance of every believer, because his gifts were necessary to complement the rest of the body. It also assured the dependence of every believer on others. Since one did not have all of the gifts, he needed his brothers and sisters in Christ. This was God's formula for unity. This design for unity, however, has been jeopardized by certain problems that have entered the life of the church.

One of the problems is found in the background of many new Christians. Many today come from a background of existentialism, which teaches that meaning and reality are only to be found in life through an "experience." Drugs, sex—anything to find purpose in a life that is at best a "sick joke." This desire to "have an experience" has permeated Christianity. In many cases it finds its expression in people looking for the more spectacular gifts of the Holy Spirit.

Another problem confronting the church regarding the gifts is that they are so often sought in a spirit of comparison and competition. I become proud because I have gifts that you lack, or I become envious because you have gifts that I lack. What originally was intended to unite us as brothers and sisters becomes the thing that divides us. The reason for this disunity is the absence of true Christian love, and this is precisely why the apostle Paul sandwiches the great chapter on love, 1 Corinthians 13, between his two chapters on the spiritual gifts.

Still another problem that we face today regarding the gifts is the tremendous feeling of inadequacy that many Christians have simply because they are not sure what their gifts are. They know that they are supposed to have gifts—at least this is what they have been taught from the Bible. But if you were to ask them what their gifts are, they would be unable to answer.

As we train young Christians to become disciples, one of our primary objectives should be to help them discover and develop their gifts, since every believer has gifts which God holds him accountable for developing and using for the sake of the body. In making disciples we are not trying to produce proficient technicians who are able to reproduce themselves by a prescribed methodology; rather, we are seeking to develop men and women who are disciples diligently exercising their particular gifts and abilities.

The Purpose and Importance of Your Gifts

To explore this subject, let us briefly study Paul's analysis of the gifts in 1 Corinthians 12.

In verses 1-11, we see the distribution and diversity of the gifts. It is frequently asked whether the gifts listed in Scripture are illustrative or exhaustive. Are they examples of a broader list of gifts? Or when you list all the individual gifts mentioned in the Bible, do you have the sum total of all the gifts that God distributes? The supporting evidence for either view is inconclusive, but I believe that the lists of gifts, such as those in verses 8-10 here, are illustrative.

This is important when helping a man discover his gifts because you have to decide whether you will confine your quest to the gifts mentioned in the Bible or whether you will view the subject more broadly. As I help people in this area, I work on the premise that any talents or abilities a person has are God-given and become "spiritual" when controlled and energized by the Holy Spirit. Other than those mentioned in the New Testament, we might look for abilities in the fields of music, writing, or art. Having helped a disciple determine what his gifts are, we can then creatively think through how his gifts can be used in accomplishing the objective of making disciples.

All that God has for me was made available through the cross of Jesus Christ; and as a believer, it is my responsibility to appropriate all that He has made available. Helping a disciple discover, develop, and use his gifts is simply a matter of helping him fulfill his responsibility to appropriate that which was made available to him through the cross of Christ.

In verses 12-31, we see the dependence of the members on the body and the body on the members. As we said earlier, the Spirit's endowment of specific gifts to each believer means that each has a uniquely significant place in the body and a complete dependence on every other believer.

This passage illustrates the foolishness of comparison. It is as ridiculous for me to compare myself with my brother as it is for my hand to compare itself with my foot. If I can understand my role in the body and the role of my brothers and sisters, I can rejoice in their success because I know that it contributes to the body as a whole.

While visiting Mexico City, I was shown a beautiful mosaic on the wall of one of the buildings at the university. The magnificent picture was composed by arranging stones of various colors and sizes in the form of a pattern. If any one of the stones had been removed, the picture would have been incomplete. The removal of your gifts from the body would make what Christ is doing incomplete.

Consider a lineman on a football team. By himself, he cannot win the game. But his blocking is indispensable if the ball carrier is going to score. An oboe in a symphony orchestra is not a solo instrument, but when played in harmony with the other instruments, it sounds beautiful.

In verses 11 and 18, we learn that God decides what function each of us is to play in the body. The feelings of inadequacy or inferiority that many Christians experience often stem from wrongly comparing oneself with others. For example, if I had been led to Christ and discipled by a pastor, I would tend to compare myself with his speaking ability and then feel quite inferior if I could not duplicate his gift. If, however, a talented musician led me to Christ and discipled me, I would be prone to compare myself with his abilities in the area of music. Again, if I could not duplicate his gifts, I would tend to experience feelings of inferiority.

We can readily see the importance of helping a man to discover his gifts and to realize their unique importance early. These gifts, whatever they are, assure his worth as an individual. It must be remembered, though, that there is no such thing as being given a gift solely for one's own personal use and edification. The very nature of the gift, whatever it may be, is such that it can be used to build up the body of Christ. The value of the gift is measured by the degree to which it contributes to the well-being of the rest of the Christian family.

Verses 25-26 teach that the body is dependent on each of the members for its proper functioning. Paul says a strange thing in Colossians 1:24: "Now I rejoice in my sufferings for your sake, and in my flesh I do my share on behalf of His body (which is the church) in filling up that which is lacking in Christ's afflictions" (NASB). What I understand Paul to be saying here is that Christ in a certain sense is still suffering. He is not physically suffering, since that was finished at the cross; but as our Head, He continues to suffer, as 1 Corinthians 12:25-26 suggests. When the head is in danger of being hit, the hand immediately responds by trying to ward off the blow at the sacrifice of itself.

Anytime one member of the body suffers for the cause of Jesus Christ, it affects every other member in the body. For example, when Jim Elliot and his four co-laborers were martyred in Ecuador, all of the church suffered. The vacancies their deaths left became our responsibility. Again, adapting Paul's illustration in 1 Corinthians 12, when one of the limbs, let's say the leg, is amputated, the body can adjust, but it cannot function as well as it could before. We say therefore that the body is handicapped.

If a person's gifts are not being used for the well-being of the body, he will not feel a part of the fellowship and will soon lose his sense of personal worth. This could be one reason organizations such as the Lions Club, the Optimist Club, and the Masonic Lodge are successful—they give their members a feeling of belonging and personal importance.

Discovering Your Gifts

Every believer needs to know what his gifts are and be using them for the well-being of the church. The church is actually handicapped if any member's gifts are not being properly applied. How then do we help people discover and develop their gifts? Let me offer four suggestions:

1. If he is a disciple, get him involved with people.

First Corinthians teaches that the purpose of spiritual gifts is to help edify the body. Gifts are never for ourselves. If a person does not know what his gift is, it may be because he is not giving himself to other people. One discovers one's gifts by selfless giving. Therefore, encourage the person you are helping to become involved in the lives of other people. As he serves others, his gifts will come to light.

2. Help him exercise any gift that you both suspect he might have.

Let's take teaching as an example. If your disciple suspects that he has the gift of teaching but is not sure, encourage him to use every teaching opportunity he can. As he teaches, it will become evident to him whether he has the gift or not.

3. *Generally speaking, a person's gift lies in the area in which his interests lie and where he can most easily exercise faith.*

Let me illustrate this by my own life. I do not have the gift of healing. When I meet sick people, I find it very difficult to exercise faith in their being made well. I do, however, preach. And whereas I am always fearful and apprehensive about standing before an audience, I can, nonetheless, muster enough faith to do it.

4. *Have him exercise the potential gift in front of people who can give an honest evaluation.*

If your disciple thinks he has the gift of teaching, let some gifted teachers evaluate him. If he thinks he has the gift of speaking, let speakers evaluate him.

A word of caution is in order here. Not having a specific gift does not absolve you of responsibility in those areas where God has commanded obedience. Let's use evangelism as an example. It may very well be that you and I do not have the gift of evangelism, but God does command that we be witnesses. His commandment is not abrogated simply because we are not gifted in that particular area. I may not be a gifted evangelist, but I am still obligated to do evangelism.

The Gifts and Calling of God

God never asks a person to do something he cannot do. There are times when He may ask a person to do something he does not think he can do. God asked Moses to represent Him before Pharaoh and the people of Egypt. Feeling very inadequate, Moses in effect replied to God, "Lord, You have the wrong man." But God assured him that He had the right man and that He would endow Moses with whatever gifts were necessary to accomplish the task.

The gifts and calling of God always go hand in hand. Most churches have some form of ordination formalities for their pastors, usually preceded by an examination council. The council examines the individual to see if he has the gifts and training necessary for the work of the ministry.

The person says to the church, "I am called of God to be a pastor."

The church, in response, says, "We must examine you to see if we concur that you have the necessary gifts and call." Ordination, then, is a recognition of the fact that the gifts and calling of God go together.

It is imperative that, early in the discipling process, the person begin to look for his gifts and develop them. His calling in life should be in harmony with whatever his gifts are. So many Christians are uncertain about their life work simply because they are not sure of their gifts. The disciple's life is a fulfilling one because he is involved in the most satisfying and exciting thing life affords, namely, helping to transform people into the image of Jesus Christ.

To experience this fulfillment, however, the disciple's life must be in accordance with the way God has made him. His function ought to be in harmony with his gifts. Whatever else the training of a disciple should include, helping him discover and develop his gifts must be part of it.

Chapter 11

MULTIPLYING YOUR EFFORTS

In 1945 a group of eminent scientists convened in a strange location, the desert of New Mexico, to test the results of many months of research. The success of their test could be of inestimable significance. It could be the key to rapidly terminating a long and costly war. The first testing of an atomic bomb was about to occur.

Atomic energy, whether in the form of nuclear warheads or plants producing valuable energy, has greatly shaped the progress of civilization since the dark days of Hiroshima and Nagasaki.

The principle underlying the mechanism of an atomic bomb is simple. Fast-moving neutrons are used to cause fission to occur within the bomb. As a neutron strikes the nucleus of a radioactive substance such as uranium, it causes it to split, forming two new, different nuclei, and in so doing to release three more neutrons. Each of these three neutrons now may strike a new nucleus and repeat the process. As each nucleus splits, energy is released. A chain reaction occurs, and the energy released takes the form of an explosion.

There is explosive power in multiplication, power that the disciple can see unleashed with the Gospel of Jesus Christ.

The Principle of Multiplication

Multiplication is one of the foundational laws of the universe. Sheep, cattle, wildlife, trees, flowers, or bacteria—every growing thing operates on a principle of multiplication. Multiplication is God's way of doing things.

In Genesis 1:28 we read, "And God blessed them, and God said unto them, Be fruitful, and multiply, and replenish the earth, and subdue it: and have dominion over the fish of the sea, and over the fowl of the air, and over every living thing that moveth upon the earth.'"

In this verse we find the first commandment that God ever gave to man, a commandment to multiply. This is about the only commandment that God has given us that we have ever been able to keep. Man has certainly multiplied on the face of the earth.

Numerically, it works out as simply as this: If parents have two children they maintain the status quo; there is no net growth in the population. When parents have three or more children, then the population begins to multiply. The more children, the faster the multiplication process.

There is a certain cost involved in multiplication. Every parent knows that reproduction is costly. The more children you have, the more it costs to raise them. There are more interpersonal relationships to cope with in the family unit. There are more decisions to be made—greater chance for disease to strike a member of the family. There is a greater chance for heartache or disappointment in one form or another. Certainly more children take more time.

For a salmon, the cost of multiplication is death. A salmon swims upstream, lays its eggs in the sand, and then dies.

Grain also dies to reproduce. Jesus said, "Truly, truly, I say to you, unless a grain of wheat falls into the earth and dies, it remains by itself alone; but if it dies, it bears much fruit (John 12:24 NASB).

Even in the development of the atomic bomb, a cost was involved. In addition to the tremendous cost in terms of money and other resources, there was the "cost" to the atom itself. It had to be split and broken in order to produce its effect.

The cost involved in multiplication can also be seen in the fact that it is initially slower than the process of addition. This is particularly important as we apply it to fulfilling the Great Commission. Let's say for example that a gifted evangelist is able to lead 1,000 people to Christ every day. Each year he will have reached 365,000 people, a phenomenal ministry indeed.

Let's compare him with a disciple who leads not 1,000 people a day to Christ, but only one person a year. At the end of one year, the disciple has one convert; the evangelist, 365,000. But suppose the disciple has not only led another person to Christ, but has also discipled him. He has prayed with him, taught him how to feed himself from the Word of God, gotten him into fellowship with like-minded believers, and shown him how to present the Gospel to other people.

At the end of that first year, this new convert is able to lead another man to Christ and follow him up as he himself has been followed up.

At the start of the second year, the disciple has doubled his ministry—the one has become two. During the second year, each man goes out and leads not 1,000 people per day to Christ, but one person per year. At the end of the second year, we have four people. You can see how slow our process is. But note too that we do not have only converts, but disciples who are able to reproduce themselves. At this rate of doubling every year, the disciple, leading one man per year to Christ, will overtake the evangelist numerically early in the 24th year. From then on, the disciple and his multiplying ministry will be propagating faster than the combined ministry of dozens of gifted evangelists.

This is not to say that there is no need for the ministry of an evangelist, but that an evangelist by himself can never complete the task of reaching a lost and dying world.

It's like the dad who offered his two sons the choice of either taking one dollar a week for 52 weeks or one cent the first week, and the amount doubled every week for 52 weeks. One son took the dollar. The other son said, "Well, Dad, I will try the penny to see what will happen." We all know who wins: the son who takes the one penny and has it doubled each week. The degree to which he wins is absolutely astounding. By the end of the year, the son who began with the penny will have enough money to live comfortably the rest of his life.

God wants the same principles that are at work in the physical realm to be applied in the spiritual realm. The reason the church of Jesus Christ finds it so difficult to stay on top of the Great Commission is that the population of the world is multiplying while the church is merely adding. Addition can never keep pace with multiplication.

Some time ago there was a display at the Museum of Science and Industry in Chicago. It featured a checkerboard with 1 grain of wheat on the first square, 2 on the second, 4 on the third, then 8, 16, 32, 64, 128, etc. Somewhere down the board, there were so many grains of wheat on the square that some were spilling over into neighboring squares—so here the demonstration stopped. Above the checkerboard display was a question: "At this rate of doubling every square, how much grain would you have on the checkerboard by the time you reached the 64th square?"

To find the answer to this riddle, you punched a button on the console in front of you, and the answer flashed on a little screen above the board. "Enough to cover the entire subcontinent of India fifty feet deep."

Multiplication may be costly and, in the initial stages, much slower than addition, but in the long run, it is the most effective way of accomplishing Christ's Great Commission … and the only way.

Quality Is the Key to Multiplication

The key to success in the multiplying process is training the disciple in depth. Each time one person fails to "reproduce spiritually," you cut your results in half.

One of Adolf Hitler's objectives was the destruction of the Jewish race, but as determined as his endeavor was, he failed. The multiplication process had gone on for too long by the time he appeared on the scene. If, on the other hand, he could have been with Abraham on Mount Moriah, and taken that knife and plunged it into Isaac, he would have destroyed the entire Jewish race with one blow.

Today, nuclear reaction is used for producing energy. Introducing a series of graphite rods into the reaction chamber controls the nuclear reaction. This slows down the multiplication process, preventing an explosion. As the church of Jesus Christ seeks to "explode" through multiplication, Satan is constantly trying to insert his "rods" to slow us down. One way Satan does this is indicated by Jesus Christ: "And the cares of this world, and deceitfulness of riches, and the lusts of other things entering in choke the word, and it becometh unfruitful" (Mark 4:19).

Note what the apostle Paul says to Timothy, his son in the faith: "And the things which you have heard from me in the presence of many witnesses, these entrust to faithful men, who will be able to teach others also" (2 Tim. 2:2 NASB). Four generations are clearly seen in Paul, Timothy, faithful men, and others also. Multiplication is assured only when there is proper training of faithful people who can carry the training process into succeeding generations.

It is easy to see that the training process needed to ensure multiplication is slow and costly. It takes a tremendous amount of time. And whenever you endeavor to insert a shortcut, you jeopardize the whole process. That is why the ministry of multiplying disciples has never been popular. Everybody likes the results it produces, but few are willing to pay the price to obtain the results.

A friend of mine and I were talking about a discipling ministry, and he said, "I am in the process of discipling fifty men right now." At that point I realized that he and I were talking about two entirely different things, for it is impossible to train fifty people at the same time. Disciples cannot be mass-produced.

While on earth, our Lord Jesus Christ was God in the form of man. He was endowed with every spiritual gift; He did not have any of our weaknesses or failings, nor did He have the heavy responsibilities of being married or running a business; His time was devoted completely to the ministry. And yet, with all of these advantages, He felt that He could effectively train only twelve; and even out of those twelve, to really major in three. If twelve was the number our Lord decided on, I doubt if we, with all our limitations, can plan to effectively disciple fifty at one time.

In Paul's second letter to the Corinthians, he explains why he has embarked on a certain course of action by saying, "Furthermore, when I came to Troas to *preach* Christ's gospel, and a door was opened unto me of [by] the Lord, I had no rest in my spirit, because I found not Titus my brother: but taking my leave of them, I went from thence into Macedonia" (2 Cor. 2:12-13).

When Paul came to Troas, not only did the Lord provide an opportunity to preach the Gospel, but also people who were ready to listen. But Paul had a problem—he did not know the whereabouts of his co-laborer Titus. Because of this, he turned down the opportunity to reach the whole city of Troas and left in search of his brother Titus.

We would tend to think he made the wrong decision because he was allowing sentiment to rule his judgment. But perhaps finding Titus was more important than preaching to the whole city of Troas just then. Why? Because if Paul reached Titus and trained him, he would double the effectiveness of his ministry, and together they could turn around and reach two such cities as Troas instead of just one.

The importance of the individual in the process of multiplication can also be seen in Acts 8. Philip (believed to be one of the deacons chosen earlier, Acts 6) went to the city of Samaria and preached the Gospel. "And the people with one accord gave heed unto those things which Philip spake, hearing and seeing the miracles which he did" (v. 6). The ministry was so successful that some of the leaders from Jerusalem came up to witness it and give it their blessing.

Right in the middle of this great evangelistic effort, the Spirit of God called Philip and sent him down to the Gaza desert to talk to one man—an Ethiopian eunuch (vv. 26-27). If Philip could multiply his ministry through the eunuch, then possibly this Ethiopian could become the key to reaching all of Ethiopia.

The discipling ministry lacks the glamour and excitement of the platform or large-meeting type of ministry. But we can hardly overemphasize the importance of investing in the right kind of person, one of vision and discipline, totally committed to Jesus Christ, willing to pay any price to have the will of God fulfilled in his life. Sticking with a person and helping him to overcome the obstacles involved in becoming a disciple is a long and arduous task.

So often I have heard the excuse, "I just don't have the gift to do this kind of ministry." Or, "God just hasn't called me to this kind of ministry." The Great Commission given to us in Matthew 28:19-20 says, "Go ye therefore, and teach [make disciples of] all nations." It takes a disciple-maker to make disciples. Historically, the church has believed that the Great Commission was not given to a select few people, but to all believers. If this is true, then all believers can be disciple-makers. Or, to put it another way, being involved in disciple-making transcends gifts and calling. Irrespective of our gifts or our calling, all men and women should be disciple-makers.

Everyone has the gifts necessary to be a disciple-maker. You may be a teacher, or a housewife, or an engineer, but regardless of your vocation, you are also to be a disciple-maker. If you are not a disciple-maker, then I would suggest that you do the same thing that Timothy did with Paul, or that Peter, James, and John did with the Lord Jesus. Make yourself available to a disciple-maker who can help you to become a disciple-maker. Latch on to him. Learn from him the "how to" involved in developing those qualities needed to spiritually reproduce yourself in the lives of others.

Every Christian should ask himself two questions: "Who is my Paul? Who is the person I am learning from; who is helping me to become a multiplying disciple-maker?" And secondly, "Where is my Timothy? Where is the person I am in turn helping to become a multiplying disciple-maker?"

Biblical Illustrations of Multiplication

Twelve sons were born to the Patriarch Jacob. The Bible tells us that they multiplied and filled the land of Egypt. "And the children of Israel were fruitful, and increased abundantly, and multiplied, and waxed exceeding mighty; and the land was filled with them" (Ex. 1:7). Jesus, likewise, chose twelve men to become His "spiritual children." He invested three years of His life in them and told them to become fruitful, to multiply, and to spread the Gospel to every creature. You and I are Christians today because twelve men caught Jesus' vision and did as He commanded. Spiritual reproduction works!

Paul's desire on his second missionary journey was to preach the Gospel throughout Asia. Acts 16:6-11 tells us that the Holy Spirit checked his attempt and finally boxed him into the city of Troas. There, Paul received the vision to go to Macedonia and preach the Gospel. So, being forbidden by the Holy Spirit to preach the Gospel in Asia, Paul and his team left and went to what is now Europe.

Now notice what happens on Paul's third missionary journey, as recorded in Acts 19. Paul is back in Asia once again, this time in the city of Ephesus. Verses 8-10 say:

> And he went into the synagogue, and spake boldly for the space of three months, disputing and per-suading the things concerning the kingdom of God. But when divers [some] were hardened, and believed not, but spake evil of that way [the Gospel] before the multitude, he departed from them, and separated the disciples, disputing daily in the school of one Tyrannus. And this continued by the space of two years; so that all they which dwelt in Asia heard the word of the Lord Jesus, both Jews and Greeks.

Here is a beautiful illustration of spiritual multiplication. Because of Paul's discipling ministry in the school of Tyrannus, everyone in the province of Asia heard the Word of the Lord Jesus. And just to make the point clear, Luke adds, "both Jews and Greeks."

Multiplying disciples is the New Testament vision and method for getting the job done. We have not taken time in this chapter to do an exhaustive study on the principle of multiplication from the Scriptures, but this might be a topical study you would like to do on your own. You will certainly find it rewarding.

Discipleship is not the ministry of any one particular organization or church. It is God's ministry. It has been on His heart from the beginning of time. Just as He set up the physical propagation of the human race on a multiplying basis, He has likewise set up the spiritual propagation of the human race on a multiplying basis. But, because of the spiritual battle involved, many would-be disciples disqualify themselves. God's cry to the Prophet Ezekiel is His cry today: "And I sought for a man among them, that should make up the hedge, and stand in the gap before me for the land that I should not destroy it: but I found none" (Ezek. 22:30). Have you heard His cry? Will you be that person? Will you be God's disciple-maker?

Chapter 12

CHOOSING A LIFE OBJECTIVE

Webster defines an *objective* as "an aim, goal, or end of action."[2] An ancient proverb states, "He who aims at nothing hits it." We need a life aim or objective.

Your life can be represented by a straight line which has as its origin your birth and an arrow on the opposite end indicating the unknown time of your death. None of us knows how long he will have in this life, but for the sake of discussion, say you have lived twenty or so years and you have approximately forty years left.

Here is the question: When you come to the end of those forty years, and you have nothing but death to look forward to and nothing but memories to look back on, what will you need to see in order for you to come to the conclusion, "My life was a success"?

I suggest that you are not ready to live those forty years until you have answered that question. Until then, your life is without direction, aim, or objective. Make sure you answer that question in specifics, because the more specific you are, the better chance you have of hitting your objective.

The Lord Jesus was able to answer positively. He said, "I have glorified thee on the earth: I have *finished* the work which thou gavest me to do" (John 17:4). Twice in the ministry of the Lord Jesus, He said, "It is finished." Once He said it on the cross, and that obviously refers to the work of redemption. But earlier He was praying in the Garden of Gethsemane when He said, "It is finished." There He was referring to His ministry. Over forty times in John 17, He refers to His disciples … they were His ministry. Repeatedly He makes reference to these twelve men who occupied three years of His life. And in that context, He says, "I have finished the work you gavest me to do." In essence, the Lord Jesus was looking God the Father in the face and saying, "O God, all that You had on Your heart for My life, I did."

When you come to die, will you be able to look God Almighty in the eye and say, "O Father, all that You had on Your heart for my life, I have accomplished. I finished the work You gave me to do"? If you cannot in integrity of heart answer yes, then whatever the price, I would strongly urge you to bring your life into alignment so that you can.

Another man who was able to claim this kind of success was the apostle Paul. "I have fought a good fight, I have finished *my* course, I have kept the faith: henceforth there is laid up for me a crown of righteousness, which the Lord, the righteous judge, shall give me at that day: and not to me only, but unto all them also that love his appearing" (2 Tim. 4:7-8). Just previously he stated, "For I am now ready to be offered, and the time of my departure is at hand" (v. 6). When your time of departure is at hand, will you say with the apostle Paul, "I have finished the race; I have done what You wanted me to do"?

When I was in college, I was looking for purpose, for meaning, for reality in my life. A giant void existed inside me. I could not put my finger on it; I did not know what it was; but I knew that the void existed. Then I met Bob, who suggested the void could be filled by the person of Jesus Christ. That God Almighty was willing to enter my life and take up residence was a brand new concept to me.

As I listened to Bob explain the Scriptures, I thought to myself, *Henrichsen, you'd be an idiot if you turned that offer down. Here is God—the Creator, the Maker of heaven and earth, the One who threw the stars into space and made everything that is—willing to enter into your life and take up residence!*

So, that night in Bob's living room I got on my knees, prayed, and received Christ. I only faintly comprehended what I was doing, but when I got up, I was a changed individual, and I have never been the same since.

The void was filled.

I began to ask questions: What really counts in life? What is really important? For what should I give my life? At the same time, I made an intensive search in the Bible for the answers.

Then I came across 2 Peter 3:10: "But the day of the Lord will come like a thief, in which the heavens will pass away with a roar and the elements will be destroyed with intense heat, and the earth and its works will be burned up" (NASB). It was the last phrase that got me: *will be burned up.*

I was an engineering major. The reason I was majoring in engineering was that I had previously worked on a construction gang in the Sierra Nevada Mountains. It was tough work, and I for one did not like tough work. Every so often I would see the engineers go by, and they did not appear to be working very hard. They would finger their slide rules, and I would think, *They've got the right job!* I decided that I would be an engineer too so that I could walk around, slide rule in hand, and tell other people what to do.

My objective—to be a civil engineer and build bridges, dams, and roads—lasted until I ran across 2 Peter 3:10. What a shock, then, to realize that everything I planned to build, God would come along and destroy! I want you to know, that discouraged me. Good grief! I did not want to build a bridge if God was going to destroy it. It was not worth it. Why give all my time and effort to build something which God had already said that He would burn?

As I continued my study, I became even more discouraged. I read, "But godliness with contentment is great gain. For we brought nothing into *this* world, *and it is* certain we can carry nothing out. And having food and raiment let us be therewith content" (1 Tim. 6:6-8). This picture emerged: I come into the world empty-handed; I build bridges and dams; God follows behind and burns them down; and when I leave the world, I leave it empty-handed. What a depressing scene!

So, I prayed, "God, I don't want to give my life to nothing. Why pour seventy years into something and then discover You will burn it, and leave me empty-handed?"

Surely there must be some purpose, some meaning, some direction for life. Surely there must be something God is not planning to burn. I continued my quest in the Scriptures. By His grace, I found two enduring things to which I could give myself.

I found the first in John 5:28-29, which says, "Marvel not at this: for the hour is coming in which [when] all that are in the graves shall hear his voice, and shall come forth; they that have done good, to the resurrection of life; and they that have done evil, to the resurrection of damnation." In the resurrection at the end time, who is going to come forth? They that have done good and they that have done evil. Everybody is going to live forever.

I have talked to people who say they do not believe in the resurrection. They do not want to be resurrected. I say, "Too bad, friend; you are going to be resurrected whether you want to be or not."

I have heard people say, "Maybe I will just be a bad guy and then God will annihilate me, and that's it." Bad guys and good guys alike are going to be resurrected. For better or for worse, people last forever.

The second thing that lasts forever is mentioned in Isaiah 40:8: "The grass withereth, the flower fadeth, but the word of our God shall stand for ever." God says, "The grass and the flowers are going to die but not My Word." There are other eternal things—God, angels, virtues such as love—but I wanted something enduring that I could grab hold of and give my life in exchange for. In setting my life's objectives, I could give myself to *people* and the *Word of God,* and know that God was not going to follow me and burn them up. He has gone on record that they are eternal. And Jesus said, "Do not work for the food which perishes, but for the food which endures to eternal life, which the Son of Man shall give to you, for on Him the Father, *even* God, has set His seal" (John 6:27 NASB).

This doesn't mean a person should not be a teacher, housewife, businessman, or even an engineer. To be involved in such a vocation may be the perfect will of God for your life. But God forbid that you should give your life in exchange for it!

The apostle Paul made tents for a living. If you had bought one of them, I am sure you would have had a good piece of equipment. Paul himself said, "And whatsoever ye do, do *it* heartily, as to the Lord, and not unto men" (Col. 3:23). But note that Paul did not have as his life objective to become the largest tent manufacturer in the Roman Empire. Rather, he invested his life in people.

Another verse really motivates me. "For the LORD's portion *is* his people; Jacob *is* the lot of his inheritance" (Deut. 32:9). You and I know people who are waiting for someone to die so they can gain their inheritance. God Almighty can choose His inheritance—anything He wants. If it doesn't exist, all He has to do is speak, and it comes into existence. "By the word of the LORD were the heavens made; and all the host of them by the breath of his mouth" (Ps. 33:6). So what does He choose? People! His people! Fantastic!

Out of everything that is or might be, God Almighty has chosen people for His inheritance. With that in mind, consider Isaiah 43:4: "Since you are precious in My sight, *since* you are honored and I love you, I will give *other* men in your place and *other* peoples in exchange for your life" (NASB). Though Israel is the subject here, and God speaks of giving others for Israel's sake, the principle can apply to us also. That is, our lives may be given for the sake of some person who is a chosen vessel (an Israel) of God. By thus winning people, we have the same inheritance, in the final analysis, which God chose for Himself. As Jesus said, "Follow me, and I will make you fishers of men" (Matt. 4:19).

Some people give their lives in exchange for money, for property, or a host of other things; yet God says these things are going to burn. But He gives us this fantastic promise that our inheritance can be the same as His. We can catch men. This is the kind of promise you will want to hold on to as long as you live. Give your life in exchange for people.

What does it mean to give your life for people? Paul writes, "So being affectionately desirous of you, we were willing to have imparted unto you, not the gospel of God only, but also our own souls, because ye were dear unto us" (1 Thess. 2:8). This means you get involved in the lives of people. When Paul went to Thessalonica, he didn't just impart a message; he gave of his very life because these people were dear and precious to him.

Giving your life in exchange for people means getting involved in the gut issues of life. This is not the same as getting involved with committees or programs. As good as these may be, they are no substitute for personal involvement in others' lives. People can be superficially involved in teaching classes, or committee work, or programs without any heart involvement. That has no cost attached to it. But when you spiritually give birth to an individual, you cannot be casual about it. You have a responsibility, it is costly, and that is why some people would rather serve on a committee than get involved in another's life.

A young boy grew up in a family with several other children. They lived in the country because his parents believed the children could better learn responsibilities there. This meant hard work for parents and children, and a life without many so-called luxuries. The family had close friends who were childless and lived in a large city nearby. Yearly these friends would take each of the children on an outing. From early morning until evening, they would see that the children had a special day: the zoo, amusement park, all they could eat at restaurants.

Riding the train back home after such an exciting day, the young lad compared the two families and their lifestyles. His family knew plain hard work, raising children, limited vacations. The others enjoyed a nice apartment, new cars, eating out, the theater after work, weekend trips, and long vacations. He decided that when he grew up, he was going to copy the lifestyle of his parents' friends. But when he got married, he saw things from a different perspective. He realized that the difference between a comfortable marriage and a costly marriage was children—reproduction.

Similarly, the difference between comfortable Christianity and costly Christianity is spiritual reproduction. It costs to become involved in the lives of people. This is why there is not a stampede to accept God's gracious offer allowing us to give our lives in exchange for people, as He did.

Another fantastic promise in the Bible is found in Isaiah 58:10-12: "And if you give yourself to the hungry, and satisfy the desire of the afflicted, then your light will rise in darkness, and your gloom *will become* like midday. And the LORD will continually guide you, and satisfy your desire in scorched places, and give strength to your bones; and you will be like a watered garden, and like a spring of water whose waters do not fail. And those from among you will rebuild the ancient ruins; you will raise up the age-old foundations; and you will be called the repairer of the breach, the restorer of the streets in which to dwell" (NASB).

This is a whole list of promises given by God, but they are all conditioned on an if. If, what? "If you give yourself to the hungry, and satisfy the desire of the afflicted." We live in an age in which there are many hungry and afflicted souls. The opportunities are legion—fantastic opportunities of getting involved in the lives of people. I find that every time an individual goes on record before God as saying, "Lord, that is going to be my objective: I am going to give my life to people; I will pour out my soul to the afflicted, and satisfy the hungry," he never wants for opportunities.

When word gets out that you are interested in people, they will beat a path to your door. Your telephone may ring a lot; your home may become like Grand Central Station; people who are spiritually needy and hungry may surround you. You do not have to be a gifted individual to get involved in others' lives. Just listen to them, that is all; you do not have to be a skilled counselor. You will be amazed how many people will want to talk to you and the things they will begin telling you: hungry, afflicted souls looking for some answers.

When you become involved with people in this way, you become a co-laborer with God in the second creation. This is the picture. God created heaven and earth. He made everything that exists. Then sin came in, and God said, "I am going to have to destroy it all and re-create. Only this second creation is going to be marvelously better than the first. So magnificent will it be, I am going to allow My people to labor with Me in that creation."

When you pour out your life into the lives of others, when you share with them the unsearchable riches of the Gospel of Jesus Christ and become involved with them in their concerns, you become God's co-laborer in a creation far greater than the first one.

Yet people turn down this opportunity day after day. A man who wanted to help some other men begin in Bible study once asked if I would help him get started. Because the men involved all had busy schedules, we decided to meet at 5 A.M. on a weekly basis in my friend's home.

The evening prior to the first meeting, I stopped by his home with the Bible-study materials to see how plans were developing. When I walked into the house, I immediately sensed that something was wrong; I could have cut the air with a knife, it was so thick. His wife was present, and before long she pointed out that she did not want those men coming and sitting on her furniture, spilling coffee and doughnut crumbs on her carpet. Furthermore, 5 A.M. was a ridiculous hour, and why should the rest of the family wake up just so these men could do Bible study. Her voice began to quiver, tears came down her cheeks, and she began to tremble, so deeply involved was she in the issue.

As I listened to her, I prayed silently, "O God, deliver me from the curse of ever believing that my living room furniture is more important than people."

Are not people's lives of infinitely more value than the furniture and carpet which God has already promised He is going to burn? Because involvement in people's lives is costly, very few take it seriously. It costs in time. Your phone will ring in the middle of the night with some distraught soul looking for answers to his needs. It will cost you your life because your life is not your own.

"Are you seeking great things for yourself? Do not seek *them;* for behold, I am going to bring disaster on all flesh ... but I will give your life to you as booty in all the places where you may go" (Jer. 45:5 NASB). Are you seeking great things for yourself? "Do not," says God, "for I am going to bring disaster on all flesh."

Jesus said, "For whosoever will save his life shall lose it: but whosoever will lose his life for my sake, the same shall save it" (Luke 9:24). I submit for your consideration that there is no greater objective in life than to give yourself for others.

STUDY GUIDE

A Thirteen-Session Small-Group Leader's Guide

Suggested Teaching Methods

Brainstorming. Announce the question or topic to be "stormed." Members make as many informal suggestions as possible, not waiting to be called on. No criticism of suggestions is allowed. List suggestions on the board; when all are in, have class evaluate and discuss the ideas. This method loosens up the group, involves non-participants, and produces new ideas.

Buzz Groups. Divide the class into groups of three to six persons, depending on size of the class. Appoint a leader for each group or let groups select their own leaders. Assign a topic to each group. Several—or all—groups can discuss same topic if necessary.

Allow five to eight minutes for discussion in the groups, then reconvene the entire class and get reports from group leaders. Jot each group's findings on the board for discussion by entire class.

Discussion. Not to be confused with *Question and Answer.* In Discussion, members react not only to the teacher but also to one another. Usually the teacher asks an open-ended question to start the discussion. A student will respond to a question, someone else may disagree with him or her, and a third person may have additional comments. The teacher is responsible for starting the discussion, keeping it "on track" by asking leading questions as necessary, and summarizing it after contributions cease. If a discussion gets out of hand and rambles, much of its value can be lost.

Group Bible Study. Each person should have his or her Bible open. Ask questions that will help the class learn what the passage says. Encourage the sharing of insights as the group discusses the interpretation of the passage and its application to current needs. Always summarize the findings or conclusions of the group. This method makes students think, it shows them how to study the Bible on their own, and it increases participation and involvement.

Interview. Ask questions—or have someone in the class ask questions—of the person being interviewed. He will ordinarily be a "resource" person—one who has a wealth of specialized knowledge on which you can draw. Alternately, an interview can be a variation on *Role-play.*

Lecture. Needs no definition! If you lecture, aim to be *interesting,* well prepared, enthusiastic, cordial, and relevant. Feel free to speak with humor when it is in good taste.

Listening Groups. Same as *Buzz Groups,* except that each group is assigned a topic to listen for as someone reads a selection—of Scripture or something else—or discusses a subject. When the class is reassembled as a whole, group leaders report, and then the entire class discusses.

Question and Answer. The teacher or facilitator asks questions, and students answer them. This method makes for good interaction between teacher and students. The teacher should word questions carefully in advance, because imprecise, confusing questions will be the death of this method, which provides involvement, guides group thinking, and keeps the class on the assigned topic, preventing "wandering."

Reading Groups. Same as *Buzz Groups* or *Listening Groups,* except that members of the group are assigned a passage of Scripture (or something else) to read and are given questions to be answered on the basis of the selection. The entire class then discusses the reports of the groups. In *Reading Groups,* there are ordinarily no leaders, though in larger groups, leaders may be helpful.

Skit. Have members read the parts of a brief script that highlights a point, provokes discussion, or presents information. This method can be fun, interactive, and provides good variety.

Role-play. Two (or more) class members, without any advance notice or written scripts, act out a situation or relationship. Give them directions as to the kind of people they are to represent and the situation in which they find themselves. They should speak extemporaneously. Follow up with analysis and evaluation by the class. This method helps people "feel" situations, gives them opportunity to try different solutions, and creates interest, especially at the beginning of class. This method also helps apply Scripture to interpersonal relationships.

Study Groups. Like *Buzz Groups,* but instead of discussing a subject, the groups study a passage, examining it for what it says, what it means, or how it may best be applied. Each group has a leader.

Guidelines for Discussion

Discussion is by far the best single method. If your group participates well in discussion, you will have little need for the other methods—which, after all, are designed primarily to stimulate discussion. If your class sits silent instead of getting into a discussion, use other methods indicated to loosen them up.

Here are a few rules for leading discussion:

1. Maintain a relaxed, informal atmosphere.
2. Don't call on people by name to participate unless you are quite sure they are willing to do so.
3. Give each person lots of time to answer a question. If necessary, restate the question casually and informally.
4. Acknowledge any contribution, regardless of its merit.
5. Don't correct or otherwise embarrass a person who gives a wrong answer. Thank him; then ask the class, "What do the rest of you think?" or, "Does anyone else have another view?"
6. If one individual monopolizes the discussion, say, "On the next question, let's hear from someone who hasn't

spoken yet." If necessary, ask the "monopolizer" privately, after class, to give other people more time to answer questions.

7. If someone asks a question, allow others in the group to give their answers before you give yours.

General Preparation

Read the entire *book,* including this *study guide.* Underline important passages in the text and make notes as ideas come to you, before you forget them. Become familiar with the study guide. A general knowledge of what is coming up later will enable you to conduct each session more effectively and keep discussion relevant to the subject at hand. If questions are asked that will be considered later in the course, you can postpone discussion until that time.

Add to your teaching notes any material and ideas you think important or of special help to your class. As group leader or facilitator, your enthusiasm for the subject and your personal interest in those you teach will often determine the interest and response of your class.

We recommend strongly that you plan to use teaching aids such as a whiteboard or chalkboard. When you ask for a number of answers to a question, as in a brainstorming time, try to write down each answer in capsule form on the whiteboard, to keep all ideas before the group. If no whiteboard is available, use a magic marker on a large pad of paper on an easel.

Once you have decided what visual aids you will use, make sure all the necessary equipment is on hand before class time. If you use electrical equipment such as digital projector, stereo, laptop, or tablet, make sure you have power available if needed.

Encourage class members to bring Bibles or New Testaments to class (or the appropriate Bible software or app) and use them throughout the class time. It's always good to have several translations on hand for comparison.

Getting Started Right

Start on time. This is especially important for the first session for two reasons. First, it will set the pattern for the rest of the course. If you begin the first lesson late, members will have less reason for being on time later. Those who are punctual will be robbed of that time, and those who are habitually late will come even later next time. Second, the first session should begin promptly because getting acquainted, explaining the procedures, and introducing the study will shorten your study time as it is.

Begin with prayer, and ask the Holy Spirit to open hearts and minds, to give understanding, and to apply the truths studied. The Holy Spirit is the great Teacher. No teaching, however orthodox and careful, can be truly Christian or spiritual without His control.

Involve everyone. The suggested plans for each session provide a maximum of participation for members of your class. This is important because:

1. People are usually more interested and engaged if they take part.

2. People remember more of what they discuss together than they do of what they are told by a lecturer.

3. People like to help the group arrive at conclusions and applications. They are more likely to act on truth if they apply it to themselves than if it is applied to them by someone else.

To promote relaxed involvement, you may find it wise to:

1. Have the class sit in a circle or semicircle. Some who are not used to this idea may feel uncomfortable at first, but the arrangement should make class members feel more at home. It will also make discussion easier and more relaxed.

2. Remain seated while you teach/facilitate (unless the class numbers over twenty-five).

3. Be relaxed in your own attitude and manner. Remember that the class is not "yours," but the Lord's, so don't get tense!

4. Use some means to get the class better acquainted, unless all are well known to one another. Perhaps each member could briefly tell something about him- or herself and share what he or she expects to get from this study.

Adapting the Course

This material is designed for use on a weekly basis, but it may be readily adapted to different uses. Those who wish to teach the course over a twelve- or thirteen-week period may simply follow the guide outline, using or excluding review/examination sessions as desired.

For ten sessions, the class may combine four of the shorter lessons into two. The same procedure could be followed to condense the study into five sessions.

An Alternate Approach

The lesson plans outlined for each session assume that class members are reading their books before each meeting. The teacher/facilitator should make every effort to spark interest in the text by giving members interactive assignments (as suggested in each session), reading aloud, etc.

When, for any reason, most of the class members will *not* have read the text in advance a slightly different procedure must be followed.

At the beginning of the period, divide the class into small study groups of from four to six persons. Don't separate couples. It is not necessary for the same individuals to be grouped together each time the class meets—though if members prefer this, by all means allow them to meet together regularly.

As teacher/facilitator of the class, lead one of the study groups yourself. Appoint a leader for each of the other groups. If people are reluctant to be leaders, explain that they need not teach and that they need no advance knowledge of the subject.

Allow the groups and their leaders as much as half an hour to study the book together. Then reassemble the class. Ask leaders to report findings or questions of unusual interest or that provoked disagreement. Ask the class the questions you want to discuss, and allow questions from your students. Be sure to summarize, in closing, what has been studied. Finally, urge each member of the class to make some specific application of the lesson to his or her life.

SESSION 1

Choosing a Life Objective / Text: Chapter 12

Session Goals

To motivate students for this study, and to help each individual examine his or her life objectives and evaluate them in light of God's Word and what lasts for eternity.

Session Overview

> *Launch:* Whiteboard illustration, visual representation of past goals
>
> *Explore*: Reading key phrases aloud, personal sharing
>
> *Apply:* Examination of current life objectives

Launch

Since your students may not receive the text until the first session, it will be important to stimulate their reading for next week, for which they will be assigned chapter 1. Do this by basing your first lesson on the *last* chapter of the text, which really brings into focus the proper motivation for discipleship and disciple-making.

1. After distributing the books, go to the whiteboard, chalk-board, or easel. Draw a straight line across the paper. Explain that life can be represented by a straight line, which has as its origin one's birth and an arrow on the opposite end allowing for the unknown time of death. Have your students imagine that they have forty years left to live, and ask: "When you come to the end of those forty years and have nothing but memories to look back on, what will you have to see in order for you to conclude, 'My life was a success'?" Don't discuss the question—just have them think about it.

Then have them read, from page 162 of the text, the paragraph beginning, "I suggest that you are not ready to live those forty years until …"

Then allow some time for the group to reflect and discuss what has already occurred in their lives and how they want their futures to look.

Move into the next section by suggesting that no matter how we describe our past, it's important, especially as Christians, to have a clear concept of our future objectives and goals.

Explore

In this section you want to draw content from chapter 12 of the text to illuminate the need to choose a life objective.

Option 1. Have someone read a section from the text in which the author shares a personal experience regarding his choice of a life objective. Ask the student to read, starting with the paragraph on page 163 that begins with, "When I was in college, I was looking for …" Conclude with the paragraph on page 165 that begins with, "The second thing that lasts forever is …"

After reading this section, emphasize the author's conclusion: Only *people* and *God's Word* are lasting, so he decided to invest his life in these things.

Option 2. Select key phrases from chapter 12 to put on the whiteboard, chalkboard, or easel so your students can grasp the basic information the author wants to communicate to them. Explain the context of each phrase within the chapter and how it relates to choosing a life objective.

Sample phrases might include:

> "But I wanted something enduring that I could grab hold of and give my life in exchange for" (p. 165).

> "When Paul went to Thessalonica, he didn't just impart a message; he gave of his very life because these people were dear and precious to him" (p. 167).

> "Because involvement in people's lives is costly, very few take it seriously." (p. 170).

> "There is no greater objective in life than to give yourself for others" (p. 171).

If you used the read aloud approach, discuss these questions:

    (a) With what parts of the author's experience can you identify? Explain.

    (b) When have you experienced similar circumstances or feelings?

    (c) What criteria does he use to determine the validity of a life objective? What are some results you can expect when investing your life in other people?

If you use the key phrase approach, have the class discuss the phrases you select and share experiences relating to them.

Whiteboard 1

This sketch and question can help your students see their need for specific life objectives.

YOUR NEXT 40 YEARS	GOAL

What will you have to see in forty years in order to conclude, "My life was a success"?

Apply

Describe Whiteboard 2 (see the end of this session), then give each student a sheet or paper and pencil and have each person reproduce the chart. In column 1, ask each to record his or her life goals, past and present, as honestly as possible. In the "Evidence" column, have everyone jot down evidence that proves his or her stated goals to be real. (For example, if a stated goal is "to succeed in business," an evidence of that goal might be "I've worked sixty hours a week for years at my job.")

Do not have them fill in the "Evaluation" column in class. Rather, encourage them to retain the chart and, after completing the course, evaluate their past goals and evidences.

Assignment

Read chapter 1 in the book, which lists nine characteristics of a person God uses. Ask your students to jot down, for any one of these characteristics, a personal experience—either positive or negative—that illustrates the need for it, and to bring these illustrations to class next week. For example, the ninth characteristic is "a disciplined life." A student could share about a circumstance in which he realized he needed discipline, or a situation in which he exercised discipline, and the results. You want your students primed with personal illustrations when they enter the classroom next week.

Whiteboard 2

Give each student a sheet of paper and have each of them reproduce this chart:

MY LIFE'S GOALS	EVIDENCES	EVALUATION
1. What were they in the past?		
2. What are they now?		

SESSION 2

The Kind of Person God Uses / Text: Chapter 1

Session Goals

To help students see that disciple-making occurs only when they involve themselves in the lives of others, and to help them understand the qualifications of a disciple.

Session Overview

> *Launch:* Discipleship multiplication
> *Explore:* Characteristics of disciple, personal sharing
> *Apply:* Discipleship covenants between class members

Launch

Launch this session by explaining the author's basic discipleship strategy: Building faithful disciples involves in-depth relationships that cannot be nurtured solely in a classroom situation. Help them understand that early Christianity spread—and Christianity is best shared today—by people totally committed to God who invested their lives to help others become committed and faithful as well.

Ask your students to estimate how many persons could be effectively discipled by an outstanding teacher who taught a discipleship course for an entire year. Suggest that the teacher could disciple a different group of students every year for twelve years, so to find out how many disciples he could produce, multiply the original estimate by twelve.

To provide contrast, suggest that this teacher invest his life in only four other persons each year for twelve years, but that, at the end of each year, each of the four persons he spent time with begins discipling four others, and so on. Calculate the total number of persons who would be discipled in twelve years using this strategy, and compare this figure with the number he could disciple in a classroom (see Whiteboard 3 at the end of this session).

In twelve years, using the second strategy, the total number of people who would be discipled is 16,777,216—a tremendously greater number than any teacher could reach alone.

Emphasize that the type of person God uses most greatly is one who invests his or her life in individuals who will in turn train others also.

Explore

Most of today's session will draw from the assignment you gave last week for chapter 1.

The author suggests that the key to a disciple-making ministry is cultivating *faithful men*. List on the chalkboard the nine characteristics of a faithful person, as provided in the text. Discuss each of the nine characteristics, and ask students to share personal experiences that illustrate each characteristic's importance. For example, one of the characteristics is "a servant heart." A student may share a meaningful experience in which someone acted as a servant toward him; another may share a time when he passed up an opportunity to serve another.

Let this sharing take much of your class time. It's important for your students to see the qualities of a candidate for discipleship in terms of personal experiences. And feel free to share your own experiences.

Apply

Since discipleship involves the imparting of a life and cannot take place solely in a classroom situation, give your students an opportunity to experience a discipling relationship.

Give your students three-by-five-inch cards, and have them write their names on them. Tell each student to write "yes" on the card if he or she wants to form a mutual discipling relationship with another class member for the duration of the course. Emphasize that writing "yes" means entering a covenant relationship with another person in which he or she assumes certain responsibilities. The partners will be responsible to pray for each other daily, to talk with each other at least three times during the week, to share with what God is teaching each other, to encourage each other, and to become sensitive to each other's needs.

Ask each person who writes "yes" to also indicate on the card three specific areas in which he or she feels a need to grow, based on the nine characteristics just discussed in class. Then take up the cards.

During the next couple of days, pair as "discipleship teams" those who responded positively. Pair on the basis of similarity of areas in which they need to grow, or pair based on geographical areas. Make sure to pair men with men and women with women. Disregard age characteristics. Notify each person regarding his partner over the phone or via email.

Assignment

Read chapter 2 in the book. If you want to assign the writing of three brief personal "stories" for use next week, do so now (see Session 3).

Whiteboard 3

The strategy of discipleship is to invest in our lives in individuals who will be able to train others also. This is one way that Christianity spreads.

Estimated number of people an outstanding teacher could disciple by teaching a class our size for one year, multiplied by twelve.
Total number of persons discipled in twelve years if teacher invests his life in only four persons each year and, if at the end of each year, each of these four persons begin discipling four others, and so on.
Figures for Each Year: 1; 4; 16; 256; 1,024; 4,096; 16,384; 65,536; 262,144; 1,048,576; 4,104,304; 16,777,216

SESSION 3

Jesus as Lord / Text: Chapter 2

Session Goal

To help your students to commit themselves willingly and totally to the Lordship of Christ Jesus.

Session Overview

> *Launch:* Communal reading of Colossians 1:13–18
> *Explore:* Writing, discussing case histories illustrating why people fail to acknowledge Jesus as Lord
> *Apply:* Review Colossians passage, prayer

Launch

Chapter 2 of the text tackles four aspects involved in making Christ Lord of our lives. Begin by stressing the importance of seeing Christ as Lord and submitting to Him. A disciple is not only a leader of others, but a follower of Christ. He must yield fully to Christ before he can be a person who leads others to maturity.

Reinforce this truth with a communal reading of Colossians 1:13–18. Perform this reading aloud in class with the entire group.

Explore

In their attempts to evangelize and disciple others, your adults may often become discouraged and frustrated over the lack of response on the part of people they seek to reach. So it's essential for them to understand the thoughts and feelings of nonChristians who hesitate to accept Christ as Savior, as well as believers who hesitate to yield certain areas of their lives to Christ. Focus the majority of the class time on the section of the text titled "Why We Don't Want to Acknowledge Him as Lord" (pp. 21–23).

1. The author mentions three reasons people fail to acknowledge Christ as Lord. Write these reasons on the whiteboard and divide into three teams, assigning each team one of the reasons. Have each team write a story or case history of a person who represents that reason for not acknowledging Christ as Lord. Or, if you assigned these stories to be written in advance (or can supply them yourself), distribute them now. The story should suggest what a person who would give this reason is like. After reading its case history, each team should discuss these questions:

    a. How does the person in our case history feel, and why does he or she feel that way?

    b. What does this person believe about Christ?

    c. What are his or her real motives for refusing to acknowledge Christ as Lord?

d. How would you answer a person who gives this reason
   for not submitting to Christ? How would you help
   him move toward acknowledging Christ as Lord?

Then reassemble the class and have each group share its case history and explain its analysis.

2. Now help your students discover what it means to acknowledge Jesus as Lord by studying the Lord's Prayer phrase by phrase.
Jesus' relationship to His Father is the model for our relationship
with Jesus. Have your adults briefly skim the section titled "What
It Means to Acknowledge Him as Lord" (pp. 23–27).

Put Whiteboard 4 on the board. Discuss the meaning of each
phrase, and let your students come up with applications for each one.
Write these applications in the right column and encourage your students to reproduce this chart on their own piece of scratch paper. To
effectively guide this discussion, you will have to carefully study the
author's comments on the Lord's Prayer. Emphasizing application of
the prayer keeps this study from becoming merely a mental exercise.

3. To crystallize the main truths discussed in today's session,
write this incomplete sentence on the board: "To me, acknowledging Christ as Lord means _____." Ask each
adult to share with the class how he or she would complete the
sentence.

Whiteboard 4

LORD'S PRAYER	APPLICATION
"Our Father"	Suggests that God cares for us as His children and that we can have an intimate relationship with Him.
"Hallowed by Thy name"	Submitting to Jesus' lordship means exalting His name above my own.
"Thy Kingdom come"	
"Thy will be done"	
"Give us this day our daily bread"	
"Forgive us our debts as we forgive our debtors"	
"And lead us not into temptation"	
"Deliver us from evil."	

Apply

Help stimulate response to Christ as Lord by briefly summarizing the section in chapter 2 titled "Why Does Jesus Want to Be Our Lord?" (pp. 27–28). Emphasize that Jesus loves us and wants to be our Lord for our own benefit. Submission is easier when we know the person in command cares for us. Submitting to Jesus as Lord should be a response to Jesus' love. Emphasize the author's point that lordship is Christ's "desire to get involved in our lives so He can tell us when it is safe to move and when it is best not to move" (p. 28). Only when people acknowledge Christ as Lord—over every area of their lives—can they effectively disciple others.

To close the meeting, encourage each student to read Colossians 1:13–18 and to pray silently about the need to make Christ the Lord of his or her own life. Encourage students to ask themselves, "Is there an area of my life in which I hesitate to yield fully to Christ's control?"

Assignment

Read chapters 3 and 4 in the book. Point out that the content of chapter 3, which describes the process of making the decision toward discipleship, has to some degree been covered in previous sessions. Encourage students to read chapter 3, but make it clear that next week's session focuses primarily on chapter 4. Encourage those whom you have paired in discipling teams to meet during the week and share their experiences and attitudes toward Christ's lordship. Suggest that they share with each other areas of need discovered when completing the chart on the Lord's Prayer.

SESSION 4

A Proper View of God and Man / Text: Chapters 3 and 4

Session Goals

To help each student gain a clear understanding of God's nature and man's nature, and to grasp the practical implications of his relationship with God.

Session Overview

> *Launch:* Brainstorming
> *Explore:* Scripture search
> *Apply:* Students select feeling words relating to God or man

Launch

A proper understanding of God and man is essential to becoming a disciple, as the author suggests in the book: "Every problem a person has is related to his concept of God" (p. 45). You want disciples to see the bigness and capabilities of God, and, in contrast, their own inadequacies apart from Him. And you want them to grasp the depth of God's love and commitment to man, despite man's tendency to go his own way.

Divide the class into two groups. Let one group brainstorm twenty-five to thirty words that describe what God is like (such as personal, powerful, forgiving). The second group can list words that describe man as we see him in relationship to God and the world (such as limited, selfish, dependent). Make two columns on the whiteboard or chalkboard and list the characteristics as each group reports its conclusions. Keep these lists on the board during the entire class time.

Explore

1. To illustrate the practical implications of God's nature in contrast to man's, present Whiteboard 5 to the class. From the text and from Isaiah 40—66 we discover that because God loves us, He is faithful to us and willing to meet our needs. And because we are needy and inadequate, we must depend on His ability to help us. It is this relationship of dependence, which gives purpose and meaning to our lives. We are linked to God by His love for us as needy people and by our trust and dependence in Him as a capable God.

2. To build a biblical picture of who God is and to share how He can be trusted, lead a Scripture search of Isaiah 40—66. Divide into three of four groups, and assign each group one of the following sections: Isaiah 40—45; 46—51; 52—59; 60—66. Have members of each group jot down significant phrases or thoughts they find that describe God. Previously, half of your

class brainstormed for adjectives describing God; this exercise will reinforce and add to that list. Reassemble and ask each group to share its findings. Add any new key words or thoughts about God to the list of adjectives put on the board previously.

Apply

1. Have everyone sit in a large circle. Point to the adjectives that describe God and ask, "How does seeing God this way make you feel?" Ask each student to think of a feeling word that goes with one of the adjectives and to share this with the group. (For example, one may reflect on God's omnipotence and conclude, "I feel *secure.*")

2. Next, point to the adjectives on the board, which describe man (written during the *Launch*) and ask, "How does seeing yourself in this way make you feel?" Again, have each student share a feeling word in response. For example, "I feel *inadequate.*"

3. To sum up this week's key truth, use Whiteboard 6. In small letters, write one or two of the feeling words shared in response to the adjectives describing man. Then take one of the feeling words shared in response to the adjectives describing God, and in large, bold letters, write it on the board so it blots out the smaller words.

Suggest that our inadequacies, fears, and doubts can be overcome by God's adequacy. Our weaknesses are swallowed up when we trust in Him as an adequate and faithful Person. Support this truth by reading aloud Isaiah 40:28–31.

Whiteboard 5

We are linked to God by His love for us as needy people and by our dependence on Him to meet our needs.

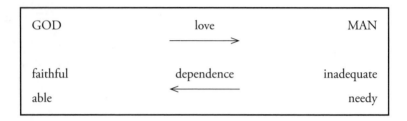

Assignment

Read chapter 5 in the book. Assign the discipleship teams the activity suggested in the last paragraph of the text in chapter 4. Each should read Isaiah 40—66 three separate times during the week. The first time, each person writes down all he or she learns about the nature and character of man. The second time, each person records all he or she learns about God's commitment to men. The third time, add to each list. Suggest that the teams meet, read the passages together, then share discoveries—or read the passage individually, then meet to share discoveries. To prepare for next week's session, ask each student to do an analysis of his own conversion experience, using these questions: "What was it that brought me to Christ? What role did other people play? What did they say that was helpful to me? Harmful?"

Whiteboard 6

inadequate, afraid
CONFIDENT!

SESSION 5

Evangelism and the Disciple / Text, Chapter 5

Session Goals

To help each student draw principles of evangelism from his own conversion experience and from John 4, and to use these principles to witness to one person this coming week.

Session Overview

> *Launch:* Personal sharing of conversion experiences
> *Explore:* Mini-lecture on John 4
> *Apply:* Witnessing to one friend during week, prayer

Launch

Being a disciple begins with a proper relationship with Jesus Christ and having the same life objectives He has. Discipling someone involves moving him or her toward maturity in the faith; yet that process begins with winning that person to Christ. In today's session, help every student see that an aspiring disciple must be willing to reach the lost.

Someone whom we personally lead to Jesus may be more teachable and more excited about being discipled by us than others would be. And often, discipling a person whom we have led to the Lord can be an easier task, since we are already aware of the needs of that prospective disciple.

Most of today's class time will draw from an assignment given last week in which students were asked to analyze their conversion experiences. Examining personal experiences can give your group valuable insights on principles important to witnessing. They can learn from the weaknesses and strengths of persons who tried to evangelize them.

1. Have everyone sit in a circle, and encourage each student to share circumstances involved in his or her conversion. Write the following questions on the board to serve as a guide for sharing:

    a. What was it that brought me to Christ?

    b. What role did other people play?

    c. What did they say that was helpful to me? Harmful?

Let this sharing use much of your class time. Try to draw out significant experiences. This exercise assumes that everyone in your class is a Christian, but if someone shares that he or she isn't, be prepared, and don't embarrass that person.

2. After everyone shares, ask your class to suggest key similarities and differences they noted in the various conversion experiences. The aim here is to draw out principles of evangelism from these similarities and differences. For example, a common denominator may be that various individuals who were responsible for leading your adults to Christ took a deep, personal interest in their lives and spent

time with them. The principle here might be stated, "Sharing Christ effectively involves building genuine friendships with others." List the principles on the board (see Whiteboard 7).

Explore

John 4 provides a striking example of Jesus' approach to evangelism. Study chapter 5 of the book carefully and prepare a five to eight minute lecture on Jesus' encounter with the Samaritan woman, in which you emphasize principles applicable to our lives today. Particularly stress the principle of tailoring one's approach to every individual, the point of leading others to a recognition of their need for Christ, and the necessity of gearing a conversation toward the needs of the other person.

As you talk, point out comparisons between the conversion experiences of class members in general and the encounter between Jesus and the woman. Encourage adults to follow in their Bibles as you share the major points to be derived from the passage. Add principles not discovered in the shared conversion experiences to the list on the board. Ask your students to think about which principles they deem most pertinent to their witnessing opportunities outside of class.

Whiteboard 7

SIMILARITIES: In our conversion experiences	Principles of evangelism drawn from our experiences:

DIFFERENCES:	

Apply

Conclude with the following summary:

"Witnessing isn't always easy, and there are many reasons people hesitate to share Christ. But one factor can motivate us and provide a context in which to share: building a friendship with the people to whom we are called to witness. When we get to know someone in depth, caring is the result. And when we learn to care for someone like Jesus cared for people, the fear of sharing will dissipate and witnessing can result. By looking at our own conversion experiences today, we've noted how other people played important roles in moving us to a decision for Christ. Now Christ wants us to be instrumental in moving others to a decision."

Close by having each person think of one nonChristian he or she sees regularly, and pray silently for God to help that person this week. If time permits, each class member can write the name of the person he or she is concerned about on the whiteboard. Each student can copy the list of names and pray for those people during the week.

Assignment

Read chapter 6 in the book. Encourage everyone involved in a discipling team with another class member to pray daily for his or her partner's attempt to witness.

SESSION 6

Getting Your Man / Text: Chapter 6

Session Goals

To help adults understand key principles on how to recruit a person for discipleship, and to encourage them to be the type of persons they want their recruits to become.

Session Overview

> *Launch:* Share witnessing results from last week
> *Explore:* Lecture, small groups, study of building process
> *Apply:* Evaluation of discipleship teams, three-by-five cards

Launch

Last week your students learned the importance of evangelism in the discipleship process, and they were encouraged to go out and share their faith during the week. Begin today's session by hearing reports from those who were able to follow through with their decision to share Christ. Urge students to share, whether or not their effort was "successful." Those uneasy about witnessing can be motivated by the successes, and those who shared but saw no immediate results can be encouraged by class members who experienced similar circumstances. Since students paired in the discipleship teams were to support one another in their evangelistic efforts during the week, give them opportunity to share what this meant to them. This should help illuminate the benefits of the discipleship teams.

Explore

A major role of the aspiring disciples in your class is to recruit other men and women to a life of discipleship. In chapter 6 of the text, the author outlines basic principles to follow in recruiting the kind of people God can use. But in helping your students discover what type of person to recruit for discipleship and how to recruit him, emphasize that they must be the kind of person they want their recruits to become.

1. Give a five to eight minute talk from the text on the eight principles to follow when seeking a person to disciple. Draw out significant points that you feel can aid the spiritual development of your particular class.

2. Next, write the eight principles on the whiteboard. Ask your class to briefly illustrate each principle so everyone can see it operating in a real-life situation. For example, the third principle is "Grow into business—don't go into business," warning against the tendency to involve oneself with more people than one can adequately handle. If a class member has ever tried to disciple too many people at one time, that person can share this experience and the results of spreading himself or herself too thin. Hearing examples of the principles at

work can give students a basis for incorporating them into their own attempts to recruit disciples. If necessary, you can refer the class to illustrations in the text that illuminate a given principle.

3. Next, focus on the fifth principle: "Development of the whole man." Point out that development of a person can be categorized into three areas: teaching, training, and building. Then have your students review this section from chapter 6 of the text, and, while they read, put Whiteboard 8 on display.

Divide your class into pairs (members of discipleship teams should meet together), and ask them to examine themselves in light of the questions on the board. Each should share with his partner his areas of need in each category of development. This can give every student involved in a discipling team valuable insight on how to "build" his partner outside of class. Encourage members of teams to discuss specifically how they can minister to each other to meet the designated needs.

Apply

To conclude, point out that having a building relationship with another person is imperative to Christian growth. One cannot become a disciple just by attending class or listening to sermons. Rather, becoming a disciple involves being taught, trained, and built up; then teaching, training, and building others.

Now that your students know more about what is involved in a discipling relationship, it is time to evaluate the discipleship teams formed after session 2. Refer to the second of eight recruiting principles in chapter 6 of the text to emphasize that a disciple can opt in or out anytime—that he or she is involved with another person strictly on a voluntary basis.

Then hand out three-by-five cards. Those who want to drop out of the discipling relationship to which they previously committed themselves can indicate their decision on the card. And those class members who didn't commit themselves previously, but who want to team up with another student now, can record their decision. This may involve some reshuffling on your part.

Whiteboard 8

Before teaching, training, and building others, your students must examine their own needs in these areas.

```
1. Do I need teaching?        In what areas?



2. Do I need training?        In what areas?



3. Do I need building?        In what areas?


```

Assignment

Read chapter 7 of the book.

SESSION 7

How to Train a Disciple: Part 1—
Follow-Up / Text: Chapter 7

Session Goal

To help your students follow up their evangelistic successes and help new converts mature in the likeness of Jesus Christ.

Session Overview

> *Launch:* Problems of new converts, describing persons who helped us grow
> *Explore:* Small groups sharing how-to-follow-up suggestions
> *Apply:* Choosing action goals for week ahead

Launch

Today's session can be especially meaningful to students who have won a person to Jesus Christ during the course of the study. They can take the practical, how-to suggestions discovered in class and apply them when relating to the new converts during the week. Students who have remained hesitant to witness can bolster their confidence by equipping themselves to relate to others. Everyone involved in a discipleship team can apply the follow-up principles.

1. Begin your session by asking everyone to share one or two major problems he or she had right after becoming a Christian. List these problems on the whiteboard.

2. Then ask each person to briefly describe the person who helped him or her grow the most as a new Christian—and have each explain what this person did to help him or her cope with or overcome the problems he or she shared about earlier.

Reflecting on the problems they encountered as new Christians will prepare your group for today's session by sensitizing them to the needs of new converts. And remembering how God used other people to help them through problems will help them grasp what their role is to be in the life of a new Christian. Before moving on, suggest that a friend who will disciple him or her is often imperative to a new Christian's growth, and that today's session can equip us in the discipling process.

Explore

Today you want to train your students to become spiritual parents who are responsible for the spiritual nurturing of new Christians. So focus the majority of your class time on a study of the four basic guidelines to helping a new convert reach maturity, included in chapter 7 of the text.

1. Put Whiteboard 9 on display. Divide the class into four groups, and assign one of the four guidelines to each group. Have members of each group brainstorm for ways in which they can apply that guideline when relating to a new convert. The book suggests several ways to apply each guideline, but group members should rely

on their personal experiences to provide additional, more specific applications. For example, the group tackling the "ensure love and affection" guideline would list many possible ways to show a new convert that he or she is loved. Students may want to skim the appropriate section in the book before brainstorming for ideas. Suggest that each group take time to allow participants to share specific experiences that illustrate an application of the guideline.

2. Have each group report their how-to suggestions to the class. Write the most significant ones on the board under the appropriate guideline. Emphasize suggestions that you feel are particularly important in discipling a new Christian. Be sure the main suggestions from the text for each guideline are included on the list.

Apply

1. You want your students to transfer the follow-up suggestions from the board to their relationship with another person. First, have each student jot down the name of a new Christian to whom he or she can begin to minister. Have each person study the suggestions on the board and write down two or three things they can do this week to help that person grow. Second, have each person who is committed to a discipling team think about the particular needs of his or her partner, and select one or two suggestions from the board to implement this week in order to minister to those needs. Then divide the class into pairs (discipling teams should stay together), and have each person pray that God will help them follow through with the applications they wrote down.

2. To close, stress the fact that a disciple who leads others to maturity must continually be progressing in his or her own spiritual life.

Suggest to your students that they must be the kind of people they want a new convert to become. For example, if one seeks to build the habits of prayer and Bible study in another's life, these disciplines must be an important part of that person's own spiritual experience. So have each student select from the chalkboard a specific area in which he feels a need to be discipled. (For example, one may want to learn how to feed himself from the Word. Another may feel a need to begin a deeper level of sharing with others.) Then each person can share with his or her partner the area in which he or she needs to be discipled. This will further equip your students to minister to each other.

Whiteboard 9

Search the text and personal experiences and suggest ways to implement each guideline when relating to a new convert.

1. How to ensure proper care and protection and deal with any trouble areas:	3. How to ensure love and affection:
2. How to ensure a proper diet.	4. How to ensure an atmosphere of acceptance:

Assignment

Read chapter 8 of the book.

SESSION 8

How to Train a Disciple: Part 2—Imparting the Basics / Text, Chapter 8

Session Goal

To help your groups discover and apply what is involved in bringing people from the initial stages of follow-up into discipleship.

Session Overview

> *Launch:* Review objectives of disciple-making
> *Explore:* Self-analysis in view of essentials, worship in the training process
> *Apply:* Planning actions for growth

Launch

Today's session focuses on the process of training a disciple. Your students will study the objectives of discipling in 1 Thessalonians 1, and learn what basic principles of Christian living to communicate in helping another reach his potential for Jesus Christ. But in class your students should evaluate their own lives in light of the basics, for they must be the type of person they want their disciples to become.

To begin, put the five objectives of a disciple-making ministry on the board (see Chapter 8). Explain each objective and suggest that we must work toward these goals in our own lives and in the lives of people we disciple.

Explore

1. Bringing people from the initial stages of follow-up to discipleship is called the training process. Help your class get a clear picture of the training process by discussing these questions: "What is the goal of training a disciple? How can a trainer contribute to another person's life? How is he limited?"

After giving your students opportunity to reply, emphasize that a trainer can, through instruction and friendship, encourage and guide a person's development. But point out that whether or not a person becomes a disciple is his own decision. A trainer provides the opportunity to learn, but he can't control the other person's feeling of responsibility or teachable attitudes, which are conducive to change and growth.

2. Most of your class time should focus on the essentials that should be present in a person's life to consider him a disciple. This section of the book lends itself to a workshop approach in class, using pairs in which each person can function as both the trainer and trainee in the discipling process. Those class members already paired in discipling teams outside of class should remain partners in this class exercise.

The Wheel illustration from the book may be copied on the board, or you may call class attention to it in the text (p. 104). This wheel illustrates the Christ-centered, Spirit-filled Christian who is living in obedience to God; its parts illuminate the basics to be incorporated into a disciple's life.

Briefly review the meaning of the hub, the spokes, and the rim; then distribute pencil and paper. Ask each student to spend ten minutes evaluating his or her own needs and goals in each of the three major areas represented by the three parts of the wheel. For example, when they come to the "rim," which represents obedient Christian living and areas of character visible to the world, they can jot down a number of character areas in which they see a need for further growth.

Put Whiteboard 10 on display and have everyone reproduce it on paper. Have everyone evaluate their "rim" qualities by specifying both where they are and where they would like to be.

3. Next have the pairs get together. Each person is to take fifteen minutes to serve as trainer to his partner (members of each pair will exchange roles after fifteen minutes). The trainer is to encourage and guide the trainee. To do this, he studies what his partner jotted down in the self-analysis just completed—particularly noting the chart involving "rim" qualities that need to be developed in his life. He asks the trainee to rate the areas of need according to priority and works with him to develop a plan that can fulfill those needs. Encourage each pair to read the section titled "The Rim of the Wheel" from chapter 8 of the text (pp. 114–116). This will show them how to develop a plan for helping the trainee build "rim" qualities or stronger "spokes" in his life.

Apply

You want each individual being trained in class to set specific actions for himself to carry out during the week, actions that can help incorporate the basics into his life. These specific actions should be part of the planning in the training process practiced in class. For example, if Joe feels a need to be in the Word, his partner may suggest that Joe read a chapter every day, memorize a verse from each chapter, and quote these verses to him next Sunday. So before class ends, be sure everyone has both clearly defined areas in which he wants to grow this week, and planned specific actions that can carry him toward his goals.

Point out that every trainee should return next week ready to share with his or her partner evidence that he or she is moving toward the goals they decided on. Emphasize that the next session will begin by having the same pairs meet. Close by having each person pray for his or her partner.

Whiteboard 10

DEVELOPING AREAS OF CHARACTER	
My present pattern in the "rim" qualities:	My desired pattern:

Assignment

Read chapter 9 in the book. Also, ask two people to prepare reports to be given in class next week. Assign one the topic of "conviction," the other "perspective." The reports should include thorough definitions of the terms, as well as brief illustrations that show each at work. The reporters can draw from chapter 9 of the book, other resource materials, and their own personal experiences. (Call or email these adults before class time to remind them.)

SESSION 9

How to Train a Disciple: Part 3—Conviction and Perspective / Text: Chapter 9

Session Goals

To help adults see their need for conviction and perspective, and to take steps to develop these qualities in their lives.

Session Overview

> *Launch:* Sharing in pairs, rhetorical question
> *Explore:* Reports, role-plays
> *Apply:* Sharing in pairs, prayer

Launch

Choosing to become a disciple is a decision that must be made on the basis of personal conviction and commitment. One should choose this option not because others suggest he "ought" to, but because he believes God is motivating him from within to do so. And since a disciple has accepted for herself the same goals Christ has, she must have perspective, or *the ability to make present decisions in light of ultimate results.* In today's session, you want adults to examine their own lives in view of these qualities. For only when conviction and perspective are embedded in their lives can they build these qualities in others.

1. As each student enters the group room, encourage that person to share with the partner he or she had in last week's session how he or she followed through on the action goals they set together (see *Apply* section, session 8).

2. When the pairs finish sharing, write this question across the top of the whiteboard: *If you experienced difficulty in implementing your action goal during the week, was it due to a lack of* conviction, *or a lack of* perspective? Suggest that conviction and perspective are prerequisites in the life of a disciple and that in today's session we will discover how to build these qualities in our lives and in the lives of people we disciple. Keep the question on the board for the entire session.

Explore

1. First, it's necessary for your students to understand the meanings of conviction and perspective. Share the reports at this time from two adults: one on conviction, the other on perspective. See *Assignment,* session 8, for details concerning these reports. After the two people share their reports, discuss:

    a. What are some personal experiences we've had that illustrate either the need for or application of conviction or perspective?

b. How can we tell whether or not a recruit for discipleship has conviction? Perspective?

c. How can we build these qualities in ourselves? In the people we want to disciple?

You can wrap up this discussion by explaining how Moses' life mirrors both conviction and perspective (chapter 9).

2. The author of the book gives four guidelines that can help adults build conviction and perspective in themselves, then in others (see headings in the text, pp. 128, 130, 133, 135). List these on the whiteboard and give a brief overview of each. Add to the list any additional guidelines discovered in the discussion just concluded. Point out that it is God who imparts conviction and perspective, but that these guidelines help us in exercising our responsibility. Be sure everyone thoroughly understands what the author is trying to say. Then study each guideline more specifically in the following way:

Divide the class into four groups. Have group 1 read the section from chapter 9 that discusses the first guideline (pp. 128–130) and make up a role-play or skit in which someone is majoring on principle rather than method, or vice versa. Group 2 can review the second guideline (pp. 130–133) and decide how to communicate it in a role-play, skit, or demonstration. And groups 3 and 4 can do the same for the third (pp. 133–135) and fourth guidelines (pp. 135–139). Or feel free to substitute one of the additional guidelines uncovered in the class discussion.

Then have each group role-play its guideline for the whole class. Every group should clearly state how its skit communicates the basic points of its guideline. But role-playing is only one suggestion. When each group first meets, you may want to suggest that its members figure out any good way to illustrate the guideline to the whole class.

Seeing the guidelines—or their neglect—in real-life situations can show your adults *how* to apply them.

Apply

Direct your adults' attention to the question you wrote on the board during the *Launch*. Now they should have a basis from which to answer this question for themselves. Divide the class into the same pairs that met the week before the training workshop, and have each share his response to the question with his partner. And have them work together to determine which of the guidelines discussed in today's session each needs to implement in reaching the action goal. Close by having each person pray for God to develop conviction and perspective in himself or herself and in his or her partner.

Assignment

Read chapter 10 in the book. Also, in preparation for next week's session, encourage everyone to study sections of Scripture relating to spiritual gifts, including: 1 Corinthians 12; Romans 12; Ephesians 4; 1 Peter 4:7–11. Members of the discipling teams can share insights gleaned from these passages when they meet during the week.

SESSION 10

*How to Train a Disciple: Part 4—Gifts
and Calling / Text: Chapter 10*

Session Goal

To help each student discover his or her own gifts and feel responsible for developing them through involvement with other people.

Session Overview

> *Launch:* Summary of teaching on gifts
> *Explore:* Self-analysis of gifts, group feedback
> *Apply:* Review, praise

Launch

The focus of today's session will be on helping students discover their gifts and special abilities so they will recognize their importance to the Body of Christ. After they discover and others affirm their gifts, they may begin to feel more responsible for other people. And knowing they have something to contribute, they may become further motivated to invest their lives in other people. This session can be especially meaningful for students who feel too inadequate to disciple others.

Begin the class by asking students to summarize the main points the author makes about gifts. Record these points on the whiteboard. Add to your students' list any significant points from the text. Emphasize the purpose of gifts, the fact that God has given everyone a gift, and how to discover a gift. Point out, as the author of the text does, that the list of gifts mentioned in Scripture may be partial and illustrative, rather than complete.

Explore

Distribute three-by-five cards and pencils. Give students five minutes to jot down spiritual gifts that they think they may have—or ways in which each person feels he or she can contribute to another person's life. Suggest that they think in terms of their past experiences (how God has used them in helping others), what they like to do, and what people have said about them.

Then have your whole group meet in a circle (if your class is quite large, divide into groups of ten to twelve). Have each person share what he or she wrote. Ask others in the group to provide feedback to his or her comments.

The feedback can be in the form of *reinforcement* ("Yes, I see that gift in you for these reasons"); *addition* ("I think you've overlooked one way in which you contribute to the Body"); or *correction* ("I'm not sure you have that gift. Would you explain again why you feel you have it?). Keep the thrust of the feedback positive and encouraging. Each class member should be noted for some way in which he or she contributes to other people. If time permits, discuss how each person's ability can be used in discipling another and in helping another discover his or her own gifts.

Apply

1. Perhaps a few of your students still aren't sure what their gifts are. Perhaps some are new to your class and church and received little reinforcement from other class members. So briefly renew how one can discover his or her gifts. Then point out that using our gifts mean becoming involved in the lives of others and helping them recognize and develop their gifts within the Body of Christ. Being a disciple involves discovering one's gifts, using them within the Body of Christ, and helping others to do the same.

2. End your session on a positive note by asking each adult to address another member of the class who has ministered to him or her during this course. In two or three sentences the speaker should tell the other person specifically how he or she ministered. ("Judy, I thank God for you because …")

3. Have each adult offer a silent prayer of praise for the gifts he or she has been given.

Assignment

Read chapter 11 in the book. Suggest that the discipleship teams meet during the week and discuss ways in which each person has already used his or her gifts to contribute to the other's growth, and new ways each person can utilize his or her gift in relationship to his or her partner.

SESSION 11

Multiplying Your Efforts / Text: Chapter 11

Session Goal

To enable your adults to grasp the reproductive potential of a discipling ministry, so they will seek to build, in depth, the persons they choose to disciple.

Session Overview

> *Launch:* Discussion starter
> *Explore:* Debate or small groups, illustrating multiplication potential of discipleship
> *Apply:* Pray about your "Timothy"

Launch

Begin today's session by writing the following statements on the chalkboard:

> "The population of the world is multiplying while the church is merely adding."
> "The depth of one's ministry is more significant than its breadth."

Ask several adults to share their first reactions to these statements. Discuss their meaning and their relation to a discipling ministry. Suggest that today's session will show how the church can multiply, instead of merely adding.

Explore

Option 1. Stage a mock debate between two group members, one serving as an evangelist, the other as a disciple. The evangelist's ministry is to win people to Christ through mass evangelism and large meetings. The discipler's ministry is to win a few people to Christ through in-depth, one-to-one relationships and to equip these people to win others also.

The proposition is: "Resolved: Mass evangelism is the most effective way of accomplishing Christ's Great Commission." The evangelist will argue the "affirmative" position; the disciple will support the "negative" position.

The adults you choose for the debate should be notified in advance so they can prepare adequately. Encourage each to use content from chapter 11 of the book as well as other resource materials. Both can construct hypothetical situations or use figures and charts to support their position.

Of course, this debate is merely a tool to creatively communicate the principles in chapter 11 of the book. You especially want adults to understand the multiplication potential of a discipling ministry as a result of it.

Point out that the way to fulfill the Great Commission isn't either mass evangelism or disciple-making. Both ministries are valid and necessary. You simply want your students to know that mass evangelism alone can't get the job done … that in the long run, discipling has more potential.

Option 2. Draw Whiteboard 11 on the board and divide your class into two groups. Have one group meet for ten to fifteen minutes, and come up with arguments to support the idea that mass evangelism is the most effective way to fulfill the Great Commission. The other group can brainstorm for reasons to fulfill the Great Commission. Encourage members of each group to construct hypothetical situations, to refer to actual events, or to use figures to support their position. Then ask each group to present its case to the whole class. Write the main arguments from each side on the appropriate column on the board. When the groups finish, emphasize the conclusion of the text: Although both mass evangelism and discipling ministries are valid and important, one-on-one discipling has more long-range potential.

Option 3. To illustrate the multiplication potential of the discipling ministry, reconstruct the activity suggested in the *Launch* section of session 2, or put this question on the board: "How many persons would be reached if *half* our class discipled one person a year for ten years, and each of these persons in turn discipled one a year?" When the correct figure is reached, write it on the board.

Sample: If there are fourteen in your class and seven become disciplers of one person a year in a multiplying ministry, the total number of persons reached in ten years would be 7,168. Here are the figures for each year: 7; 14; 28; 56; 112; 224; 448; 896; 1,792; 3,584; 7,168.

Compare the number you get to the difference in your church membership ten years ago and now. (This may require examining church records.) While your church has probably added members, it probably doesn't show a multiplication close to the number half your class could disciple in ten years.

Option 4. Next, discuss: "What is the key to success of a multiplication ministry?" After allowing several adults to share their ideas, refer them to the paragraph in chapter 11 of the book that begins with, "The discipling ministry lacks the glamour …" (p. 156). Point out that *quality* is the key—finding a person to disciple who will in turn disciple others, and being the type of person who can effectively train another.

Whiteboard 11

Both mass evangelism and one-to-one discipling ministries are important. But today's session should help your adults see the greater long-range potential of an in-depth discipling relationship.

MOST EFFECTIVE WAY TO FULFILL THE GREAT COMMISSION…	
Mass evangelism … or	in-depth discipling relationship

Apply

Most of your students should be involved in a discipling team. Encourage the adults involved to view their partners as "Pauls" who build them.

And suggest that this leaves them with the responsibility of finding "Timothys" (others they can disciple). Close by having everyone pray silently; ask God to lead them in the days ahead to their Timothys.

Assignment

Before your adults leave, emphasize that in session 12, those on the discipling teams will have opportunity to share some of what they have been learning, for everyone's benefit. Make copies of the six questions from the *Explore* section of session 12 and give a copy to every student on a discipling team. This will equip them to enter the classroom next week ready to share. Encourage partners to meet during the week and exchange their personal answers to the questions. Since the principles of chapter 12 are crucial to proper motivation, ask the students to read chapter 12 again carefully and prayerfully, even though your opening lesson was also based on this chapter.

SESSION 12

Experiences in Discipling / Text: Chapter 12

Session Goal

To allow each student to learn from and become motivated by his classmates' experiences in discipling teams, and to review principles learned.

Session Overview

> *Launch:* Brief review of course
> *Explore:* Personal sharing by discipling teams
> *Apply:* Commitment to discipling lifestyle

Launch

What your adults have learned in class and in the book about discipleship is important, but you're aware that discipling takes place not in a classroom but in relationship to another in real-life situations. That's why in session 2 you gave every student an opportunity to begin a discipling relationship outside the classroom with another class member. This has provided a context in which students could apply and experience the principles of discipleship covered in class. We have called these student pairs "discipling teams."

We may learn as much or more from the experiences of students involved in the teams as from an extensive review of every chapter in the text. But before these teams share, use whiteboard 12 to give a five to eight minute review of the main points covered over the past eleven weeks. Save time by having these points written on the board in advance. Add any other key truths you feel your adults should remember to the list. You will need to review the whole text and think in terms of your people's particular needs when selecting main points to add. This will give students a picture of the whole discipling process. But then suggest that a more meaningful review may be gleaned from the experiences of the discipling teams.

Explore

With members of the discipling teams sitting together, arrange your class in a large circle. (If your class is quite large, divide into two or three groups to allow for in-depth sharing by each team.)

Introduce each discipling team and have each partner respond to the questions on the following list. Encourage members of each team to share specific experiences they've had together in response to the questions. (You should have given each person a copy of these questions ahead of time. See *Assignment,* session 11). Let each team respond to some or all the questions before moving to the next team. And if time permits, allow other class members to ask each team additional questions. You may have to set a time limit for each team so everyone will have an opportunity to share.

Have these questions in front of everyone by making copies of them and distributing them, or displaying them on the board.

1. How has your partner helped you grow as a Christian? (Share anecdotes and specific qualities he or she has helped build in you.)
2. What discipling skills has he or she imparted to you, and how did he or she impart them?
3. What mistakes have you made, both as a disciple and a disciple that you have learned from?
4. What have you learned from this relationship about the costs of discipleship?
5. What has been the most rewarding aspect of this relationship? The most difficult or frustrating?
6. Based on your experiences together, what suggestions would you make to someone wanting to enter a discipling relationship?

Whiteboard 12

Have this summary of main points from the text written ahead of time on the board.

KEY TRUTHS FROM COURSE
1. Giving our lives for others is life's greatest objective.

2. The key to a discipling ministry is faithful men and women who yield fully to Christ's lordship.
3. The process of discipling begins with winning others to Christ.
4. Discipling involves a development of the whole man.
5. Discipling involves in-depth personal relationships in which we train others according to their needs.
6. We must be the type of people we want our disciples to become.
7. Help aspiring disciples discover and use their spiritual gifts.
8. A reproductive one-to-one ministry has the greatest long-range potential in fulfilling the Great Commission.
[Add a few of your own below]
9.
10.
11.

Apply

You want their involvement in a discipling team to launch a new, discipling life-style for your adults. Today's session should make your adults more sensitive to the commitment and the personal sacrifice required in a disciple-making ministry. Close by having them ponder this question: "Knowing what is involved, are you ready to commit yourself *permanently* to a discipling life-style?"

Encourage everyone who can honestly say "yes" to look forward to the last session next week, in which they may plan the months ahead in light of their objective to invest their lives in people. Suggest that students who are hesitant to become disciple-makers read chapter 12 of the text *again* so that they might make their decision "with eternity's values in view."

Assignment

Just as you did at the end of session 11, encourage every adult to pray about one person outside of class whom he or she could disciple. This person may be a contact at work or a neighbor. This person may be a committed Christian who is eager to be trained and built by another, or it may be a nonChristian whom a student wants to evangelize, then disciple. Emphasize that everyone should have a "Timothy" on his or her mind when he or she enters the classroom next week. Members of discipling teams should meet and pray together about this need during the week.

SESSION 13

Reaching Out to Your "Timothy"

Session Goal

To help every student discern the personal needs of his or her "Timothy" and plan specific steps to meet those needs.

Session Overview

> *Launch:* Discerning needs of "Timothy"
> *Explore:* Small-group sharing about persons to be discipled, prayer
> *Apply:* Stating action goals to meet needs of "Timothy"

Launch

Hopefully, every adult who attends today's session will be ready to begin discipling another person in the weeks ahead. So it's important for them to evaluate how well they know the person they want to disciple—since discipling involves in-depth relationships—and then to plan specific action goals based on the needs of their "Timothy."

Distribute index cards and ask every adult to jot down the name of the person he or she wants to disciple. Next have your students list several personal needs of their "Timothys." Remind your adults that though discipling connotes leading someone who is already a Christian to maturity, they can choose to evangelize a nonChristian who would have potential for discipleship.

Explore

Next break up into groups of six to eight. Have each person in the group share in the following manner concerning the person he or she wants to disciple (put these instructions on the board):

1. Tell what the person is like—his or her characteristics, interests, background.
2. Describe some of his or her current personal needs.
3. Share what your relationship has been with him or her until now.
4. Explain why you selected him or her as your disciple-to-be.
5. Share the biggest problem you foresee in reaching or discipling this person.

After each person shares, have others in this group suggest specific actions he or she should take in reaching out to his or her "Timothy." Their suggestions should be based on the personality and needs of the disciple-to-be and on principles learned in this course. Have others in the group pray for each person after he or she shares.

This exercise helps each adult plan his or her discipling ministry based on the needs of the other person. And your students can learn how to reach out from the feedback and shared experiences of others in the group. Allow this group exercise to take most of the class time.

Apply

At the beginning of today's session, you asked everyone to jot down needs of the person they want to disciple. In the groups, each adult shared these needs and received from others in the group suggested actions to take when reaching out. To help everyone apply the suggestions, have every student jot down, on the same index card on which he or she earlier described the needs of "Timothy," one or two specific ways he or she can help meet those needs.

Before closing, encourage everybody who joined a discipling team during the course to maintain a close relationship with their partners in the future. The support their partners provide can further equip them to disciple others.

NOTES

1. John W. Gardner, *Excellence* (New York: W. W. Norton & Company, Inc., 1995), 155-156.

2. *Merriam-Webster's Collegiate Dictionary*, 11th ed., s.v. "objective."